First World War
and Army of Occupation
War Diary
France, Belgium and Germany

41 DIVISION
123 Infantry Brigade
Queen's (Royal West Surrey Regiment)
11th Battalion
3 May 1916 - 31 October 1917

WO95/2638/4

The Naval & Military Press Ltd
www.nmarchive.com
Published in association with The National Archives

Published by

The Naval & Military Press Ltd

Unit 10 Ridgewood Industrial Park,

Uckfield, East Sussex,

TN22 5QE England

Tel: +44 (0) 1825 749494

www.naval-military-press.com

www.nmarchive.com

This diary has been reprinted in facsimile from the original. Any imperfections are inevitably reproduced and the quality may fall short of modern type and cartographic standards.

© **Crown Copyright**
Images reproduced by permission of The National Archives, London, England, 2015.

Contents

Document type	Place/Title	Date From	Date To
Heading	WO95/2638/5 11/Queen's (R.W. Surrey) May 16-Oct 17		
War Diary	Aldershot	03/05/1916	03/05/1916
War Diary	Strazeele	07/05/1916	31/05/1916
Miscellaneous	March Table 11th Queen's Appendix I		
War Diary	Le Bizet	01/06/1916	07/06/1916
War Diary	Trenches	08/06/1916	12/06/1916
War Diary	Le Bizet	13/06/1916	16/06/1916
War Diary	Trenches,	17/06/1916	26/06/1916
War Diary	Le Bizet	26/06/1916	29/06/1916
Miscellaneous	11th (S) Bn. "The Queen's (R.W.S.) Regt.		
Map			
War Diary	Le Bizet	03/07/1916	03/07/1916
War Diary	Trenches	04/07/1916	28/07/1916
Miscellaneous	Weekly Strength Return.	08/07/1916	08/07/1916
Miscellaneous	Details.		
Miscellaneous	Weekly Strength Return.	15/07/1916	15/07/1916
Miscellaneous	Weekly Strength Return.	22/07/1916	22/07/1916
Miscellaneous	Weekly Strength Return.	29/07/1916	29/07/1916
Map			
War Diary	Trenches	01/08/1916	07/08/1916
War Diary	Le Bizet	09/08/1916	24/08/1916
Miscellaneous	11th (S) Bn. "The Queen's Regt. Weekly Strength Return.	06/05/1916	06/05/1916
Miscellaneous	Weekly Strength Return.	12/08/1916	12/08/1916
Miscellaneous	Weekly Strength Return.	19/08/1916	19/08/1916
Miscellaneous	Weekly Strength Return.	26/08/1916	26/08/1916
War Diary	Bussus-Bussuel	01/09/1916	10/09/1916
War Diary	Delville Wood	11/09/1916	13/09/1916
War Diary	Montauban Alley	14/09/1916	16/09/1916
War Diary	Flers	16/09/1916	30/09/1916
Miscellaneous	Weekly Strength Return	02/09/1916	02/09/1916
Miscellaneous	11th (S) Bn. The Queen's (R.W.S) Reg. Weekly Strength Return	09/09/1916	09/09/1916
Miscellaneous	11th (S) Bn. The Queen's (R.W.S) Reg. Weekly Strength Return	16/09/1916	16/09/1916
Miscellaneous	11th (S) Bn. The Queen's (R.W.S) Reg. Weekly Strength Return	23/09/1916	23/09/1916
Miscellaneous	11th (S) Bn. The Queen's (R.W.S) Reg. Weekly Strength Return	30/09/1916	30/09/1916
Operation(al) Order(s)	123rd Infantry Brigade Order No. 31	14/09/1916	14/09/1916
Miscellaneous	Appendix "A" Assembly		
Miscellaneous	11th (S) Bn. "The Queen's" Regiment.	19/09/1916	19/09/1916
Miscellaneous	Orders 2nd The Event Of Every Counter Attack		
Miscellaneous	Time Table Of Attack.		
Miscellaneous	Appendix. B.		
Miscellaneous	Table-3 Situation And Contents Of Dumps. Situation.		
Map			
War Diary	Flers	01/10/1916	01/10/1916
War Diary	Pommiers	02/10/1916	02/10/1916

War Diary	Mametz Wood	07/10/1916	07/10/1916
War Diary	Flers Trenche	07/10/1916	09/10/1916
War Diary	Flers	10/10/1916	10/10/1916
War Diary	Mametz Wood	13/10/1916	13/10/1916
War Diary	Dernancourt	17/10/1916	17/10/1916
War Diary	Limeux	19/10/1916	19/10/1916
War Diary	Godewaersvelde	22/10/1916	22/10/1916
War Diary	Chippewa Camp	23/10/1916	23/10/1916
War Diary	Trenches	28/10/1916	28/10/1916
Miscellaneous	All Coys Quince	08/10/1916	08/10/1916
Map	App II		
Miscellaneous	11th (S) Bn The Queens (R.W.S) Regt. Weekly Strength Return	07/10/1916	07/10/1916
Miscellaneous	11th (S) Bn The Queens (R.W.S) Regt. Weekly Strength Return	14/10/1916	14/10/1916
Miscellaneous	11th (S) Bn The Queens (R.W.S) Regt. Weekly Strength Return	21/10/1916	21/10/1916
Miscellaneous	11th (S) Bn The Queens (R.W.S) Regt. Weekly Strength Return	28/10/1916	28/10/1916
War Diary	Reninghelst	02/11/1916	03/11/1916
War Diary	Trenches	04/11/1916	08/11/1916
War Diary	Reninghelst	09/11/1916	27/11/1916
Miscellaneous	11th (S) Bn. The Queens (RWS) Regt. Weekly Strength Return.	04/11/1916	04/11/1916
Miscellaneous	11th (S) Bn. The Queen's (RWS) Regt. Weekly Strength Return.	11/11/1916	11/11/1916
Miscellaneous	11th (S) Bn. The Queen's (RWS) Regt. Weekly Strength Return.	18/11/1916	18/11/1916
Miscellaneous	11th (S) Bn. The Queen's (R.W.S.) Regt. Weekly Strength Return.	25/11/1916	25/11/1916
War Diary	Trenches	02/12/1916	03/12/1916
War Diary	Reninghelst	08/12/1916	28/12/1916
Miscellaneous	11th Bn "The Queens (RWS) Regt. Weekly Strength Return.	02/12/1916	02/12/1916
Miscellaneous	11th Bn The Queens (R.W.S) Regt. Weekly Strength Return.	09/12/1916	09/12/1916
Miscellaneous	11th Bn The Queens (R.W.S) Regt. Weekly Strength Return.	16/12/1916	16/12/1916
Miscellaneous	11th Bn The Queens (R.W.S) Regt. Weekly Strength Return.	23/12/1916	23/12/1916
Miscellaneous	11th Bn The Queens (R.W.S) Regt. Weekly Strength Return.	30/12/1916	30/12/1916
War Diary	Reninghelst	01/01/1917	01/01/1917
War Diary	Trenches	02/01/1917	02/01/1917
War Diary	Reninghelst	07/01/1917	07/01/1917
War Diary	Trenches	14/01/1917	19/01/1917
War Diary	Reninghelst	21/01/1917	21/01/1917
War Diary	Trenches	27/01/1917	27/01/1917
Miscellaneous	11th Bn "The Queen's (R.W.S.) Regt. Weekly Strength State.	07/01/1917	07/01/1917
Miscellaneous	11th Bn "The Queen's (R.W.S.) Regt. Weekly Strength State.	13/01/1917	13/01/1917
Miscellaneous	11th Bn "The Queen's (R.W.S.) Regt. Weekly Strength Return.	20/01/1916	20/01/1916
Miscellaneous	11th Bn "The Queen's (R.W.S.) Regt. Weekly Strength Return.	27/01/1917	27/01/1917

Type	Description	Start	End
War Diary	In The Field	01/02/1917	26/02/1917
Miscellaneous	11th Bn The Queen's (R.W.S). Regt. Weekly Strength Return.	03/02/1917	03/02/1917
Miscellaneous	11th Bn The Queen's (R.W.S). Regiment. Weekly Strength Return.	10/02/1917	10/02/1917
Miscellaneous	11th Bn. "The Queen's (R.W.S). Regt. Weekly Strength Return.	16/02/1917	16/02/1917
Miscellaneous	11th Bn. "The Queen's (R.W.S). Regt. Weekly Strength Return.	24/02/1917	24/02/1917
War Diary	Reninghelst	01/03/1917	01/03/1917
War Diary	Spoil Bank (B.H.Q.). I.33. 1.0.6	04/03/1917	24/03/1917
War Diary	Spoil Bank	29/03/1917	29/03/1917
Miscellaneous	11th Bn. The Queen's (R.W.S) Regt. Weekly Strength Return.	03/03/1917	03/03/1917
Miscellaneous	11th Bn. The Queen's (R.W.S) Regt. Weekly Strength Return.	10/03/1917	10/03/1917
Miscellaneous	11th Bn. The Queen's (R.W.S) Regt. Weekly Strength Return.	17/03/1917	17/03/1917
Miscellaneous	11th Bn. The Queen's (R.W.S) Regt. Weekly Strength Return.	24/03/1917	24/03/1917
Miscellaneous	11th Bn. The Queen's (R.W.S) Regt. Weekly Strength Return.	31/03/1917	31/03/1917
War Diary		01/04/1917	30/04/1917
War Diary	Reninghelst	01/05/1917	01/05/1917
War Diary	In The Line	03/05/1917	12/05/1917
War Diary	Reninghelst	19/05/1917	19/05/1917
War Diary	In The Line	26/05/1917	26/05/1917
War Diary	Reninghelst	31/05/1917	31/05/1917
Heading	War Diary 11th (S) Bn "The Queen's (R.W.S) Reg. June 1st-30th 1917		
War Diary	Reninghelst Belgium	01/06/1917	04/06/1917
War Diary	Sheet 28 SW 2.	05/06/1917	05/06/1917
War Diary	O 3a 79 1/2	06/06/1917	07/06/1917
War Diary	Damstrasse	07/06/1917	12/06/1917
War Diary	Voormezeele	13/06/1917	18/06/1917
War Diary	Old French Trench	19/06/1917	30/06/1917
Operation(al) Order(s)	Operation Order No. 9. By Major H. Wardell. Commanding 11th (S) Battn. "The Queen's" (R.W.S) Regiment. Appendix I		
Miscellaneous	Duplicates		
Operation(al) Order(s)	Operation Order No 9 By Major H. Wardell. Commanding 11th (S) Battn. "The Queen's" (R.W.S) Regiment.		
Miscellaneous	Additions And Alterations To Operation Order No. 9		
Miscellaneous			
Map			
Miscellaneous	Appendix II		
War Diary	Mont De Cats	01/07/1917	07/07/1917
War Diary	Westoutre	21/07/1917	23/07/1917
War Diary	De-Zon	24/07/1917	25/07/1917
War Diary	Imperial Trench	25/07/1917	31/07/1917
War Diary	Battle Field	31/07/1917	31/07/1917
Miscellaneous	Operation Order by Lieut Colonel R. Otter M.C. Commanding 11th (S) Battn. "The Queen's" (R.W.S) Rgt.	19/07/1917	19/07/1917
War Diary		01/08/1917	31/08/1917

War Diary		01/09/1917	30/09/1917
War Diary	Fort Des Dunes	01/10/1917	05/10/1917
War Diary	Witteburg	06/10/1917	15/10/1917
War Diary	La Panne	16/10/1917	31/10/1917

WO95/2638 (5)
11/Queen's (R.W. Surrey)
May '16 — Oct '17

WAR DIARY
or
INTELLIGENCE SUMMARY

(Erase heading not required.)

Army Form C. 2118

VOLUME Nº I
5 5/16 - 31 5/16
11th W Surrey
Vol I

Instructions regarding War Diaries and Intelligence Summaries are contained in F. S. Regs., Part II. and the Staff Manual respectively. Title Pages will be prepared in manuscript.

Place	Date	Hour	Summary of Events and Information	Remarks and references to Appendices
Aldershot	5th May 1916	5 pm	The battalion, including command of Lieut Col. H.B. Bircraly D.S.O. left Aldershot for Southampton the port of embarkation. The following officers were present with the battalion :— Lieut. Col. H.B. Bircraly D.S.O. (in command) Major H. Hardie (2nd in command) Major R.C. Graham Clark " R. Chick (Durham Light Infantry) Captain C.J. Hogan " F.C. Reynolds " P.P. Langley " T. Kelly " Hillier C. Sharpe Lieut E.A. Bourdure A & S Cox	

WAR DIARY
or
INTELLIGENCE SUMMARY
(Erase heading not required.)

Army Form C. 2118

Instructions regarding War Diaries and Intelligence Summaries are contained in F.S. Regs., Part II. and the Staff Manual respectively. Title Pages will be prepared in manuscript.

Place	Date	Hour	Summary of Events and Information	Remarks and references to Appendices
			Lieut. J.P.H. Cookson	
			A.R. Hadley	
			H. McDonald (Transport Officer)	
			J.H. Strange	
			R.V. Peddon	
			M.C. Porter	
			J.P. White (R.A.M.C.) Lee. Lieut. O.J. Partington	
				A.E. Pearman
				F.B. Smith
				J. Hannaford (Signalling Officer)
			Lee. Lieut. H.H.S. Chapman	
			H.N.L. Cook	C.H. Wiley
			J.A. Cowan	D.C.H. O'Byrne
			H.O. Head	Lieut. & Quarter-master D.W. Jordan
			J.M. Henri	
			C.A. Dunstup	Regimental Sergt. Major A.C. Middleton
			H.L. Reif	
			R. Dove	Other Ranks – 924.

Army Form C. 2118

WAR DIARY
or
INTELLIGENCE SUMMARY
(Erase heading not required.)

Instructions regarding War Diaries and Intelligence Summaries are contained in F. S. Regs., Part II. and the Staff Manual respectively. Title Pages will be prepared in manuscript.

Place	Date	Hour	Summary of Events and Information	Remarks and references to Appendices
STRAZEELE	7/5/16		After a delay of 24 hours, owing to a fog, the battalion, having embarked on S.S. CAESAREA, arrived at HAVRE in the early hours of 5th May 1916. Left HAVRE on the evening of 5th May by train, arriving at GODEVAERSVELDE afternoon 6th May - thence by march route to STRAZEELE, where it was billeted in 5 separate farm houses. The training of the battalion was continued without delay - chiefly in various phases of trench warfare	R.C./Capt.
	11/5/16		A party of 5 officers & 20 NCOs proceeded to the trenches for a course of 2 days -	R.C./Capt.
	13/5/16		A party of 5 officers and 20 NCOs of B Coy proceeded to trenches for a course of 2 days -	R.C./Capt.
	14/5/16		A party of 5 officers and 20 NCOs of C Coy proceeded to trenches for a course of 2 days	R.C./Capt.

WAR DIARY
or
INTELLIGENCE SUMMARY
(Erase heading not required.)

Army Form C. 2118

Place	Date	Hour	Summary of Events and Information	Remarks and references to Appendices
	18/5/16		A party of 7 officers, including C.O. and Adjutant, and 20 NCOs proceeded to the trenches for a course of 2 days. As near to each of these parties, 2 or 3 specified NCOs were added. As each day party proceeded to the identical trenches that the company would take over on relief, much useful and practical knowledge was thereby obtained.	R.C. Smith Capt APP. 7. R.C. Smith Capt
STRAZEELE	30/5/16	5 p.m.	Battalion left STRAZEELE for NOOTE BOOM, where it was billetted for the night and following day. The Belles met with of the 3 battalions in the left	
	31/5/16	2 p.m.	left for LE BIZET. The Belles met with of the first line of trenches. Arrived in sub-sector of the brigade sector of the first line of trenches. Arrival in LE BIZET at 8 p.m. without opposition, which was found, owing to rumours having spread placards in the vicinity to the effect that they were aware of the coming relief. The transport was billetted near PLOEGSTEERT.	R.C. Smith Capt

R.C.Smith Capt for Lt.Col.
Cmdg 11th Bn Middlesex Regt.

1/6/16

Appendix 2

MARCH TABLE   11th Queen's.

DATE.	UNIT.	FROM	TO	ROUTE.	TIME	DISTANCE.	REMARKS.
29th May.	11th Queen's	STRAZEELE	NOOTE BOOM.	MERRIS-South to Cross Roads F.13.a.6.2.(Sheet 36A) -HTE.MAISON - NOOTE BOOM.	Leave present billeting area at 5 p.m.	5 miles.	A Motor Lorry will carry the Blankets.These will be collected at Battalion H.Q.ready to be moved. A cycle orderly will return to Bde. H.Q. BAILLEUL when he has ascertained the position of his own Battalion H.Q. The Battalion is not to arrive at NOOTE BOOM before 6.30 p.m.
31st May.	11th Queen's	NOOTE BOOM	LE BIZET	NOOTE BOOM-Road Junction A.7.d.3.8. (Sheet 36)-Road Junction A.2.c.8.1. (Sheet 36) - STEENWERCK-TROIS ARBRES-PAPOT - NIEPPE-PONT DE NIEPPE -LE BIZET.	Leading Platoon to pass road junction A.7.d.3.8. at 2 p.m.	10 miles to LE BIZET 8 miles to PONT-DE NIEPPE.	1st Platoon to arrive at H.Q. 1st.S.A.Inf.Bde.at 5.30 p.m. A motor lorry will carry blankets right up to LE BIZET.arrangements must be made to show them where they are to be taken to. A billeting party of 1 officer, 2 N.C.O's and 16 men will be sent on to the 10th R.W.Kent Regt.on the 28th. They will go with that Regiment to LE BIZET where they will remain.On the afternoon of the 31st they will meet their Platoons on the nmain BAILLEUL Road at PONT DE NIEPPE and conduct each Platoon straight to its billet.

WAR DIARY or INTELLIGENCE SUMMARY

Army Form C. 2118

11TH BN THE QUEEN'S REGT.
VOLUME No II Vol 2 June
1/6/16 — 30/6/16

Place	Date	Hour	Summary of Events and Information	Remarks and references to Appendices
LE BIZET	1–4th June		Every available man employed in Working Parties, working on various means of approach principally BORDER AVENUE, BARKENHAM AVENUE and SMYTH AVENUE. On the night of June 3/4th, the first casualty occurred No 9/11646 Private BARTLETT F.W. being killed whilst on one of these working parties. On June 3rd, 2 more men were wounded.	For Defence Scheme and Sketch see APP II
LE BIZET	5th June 8.10 p.m.		The relief of the 10th Bn. Royal West Kent Regiment began in the front line trenches. The platoons were led to their places in the line by Guides of the relieved regiment, at intervals varying from 5–10 minutes. The completion of the relief was reported at 12.20 a.m. 6th June. Attached is a rough plan of the trenches taken over, shewing portions occupied by the various companies. Also a scheme for the defence of line, which was duly carried out.	
	6th June		Quiet day. Little sniping at night. Casualties. 1 killed (accidental) 1 wounded	
	7th June		Quiet. About 20 shells were fired into DALPIERRE FARM. Casualties. Nether 1/wounded	

WAR DIARY
or
INTELLIGENCE SUMMARY
(Erase heading not required.)

Army Form C. 2118

Place	Date	Hour	Summary of Events and Information	Remarks and references to Appendices
Trenches	8th June		Nothing worthy of report. Usual sniping carried out throughout the night. Casualties – 2 slightly wounded.	
	10th June	4.30 p.m.	The enemy bombarded GLASGOW REDOUBT with aerial torpedoes and 16 pounders. In retaliation for an intense bombardment of ours they were employing ("Pom"). 124th Infy Brigade. Casualties – Capt C.J. Hogan slightly wounded, O.R. 1 killed and 3 wounded. At 12 midnight 10th/11th June a party of 3 men under Lieut Milne and 1 officer and 2 men of the Australian Tunnelling Company came to the RED HOUSE, C.4.d. 1 & 2 (Sheet 36.N.W.2) where it was supposed that tunnelling operations were in progress. It was found the unfounded and some flares up with 50 lbs of ammonal.	
	11th June		Very quiet day. Nothing to report.	
	12th June	11.30 p.m.	Battalion was relieved by the 10th Bn Royal West Kent Regiment. Casualties 2 men wounded.	
	13th June	11 p.m.	Every available man on working parties.	
L.13/12.C.7	14th June		Time performed 1 hour – Henceforth relieves will be British Summer Time. Relief of trenches trenches complete.	
	17th June	12 midnight	Casualties 2 men wounded, 1 accidentally, on working parties.	

WAR DIARY
or
INTELLIGENCE SUMMARY
(Erase heading not required.)

Army Form C. 2118

Instructions regarding War Diaries and Intelligence Summaries are contained in F. S. Regs., Part II. and the Staff Manual respectively. Title Pages will be prepared in manuscript.

Place	Date	Hour	Summary of Events and Information	Remarks and references to Appendices
Trenches	17th		During the course of the day, some 15 shells fell in GLENCORSE REDOUBT and several torpedoes, but with little success. Quiet. Casualties 1 killed and 1 wounded (accidental)	
	18th		During the night, all the enemy wire opposite our trenches was examined. Wiring parties were now sent out nightly, and grass-cutting parties outside our wire, infront 15 yards in depth, commencing from 5 yards outside our wire. Rendered difficult by numerous trip wires which have been thrown into No Man's Land. Sniping increased a good deal, and enemy's artillery appear more active. Casualties 3 killed 1 wounded	
	19th		Slightly increased activity in artillery and sniping. Nothing to report. Wiring and grass-cutting continued under cover of darkness. 3 men slightly wounded.	
	20th		Quiet. 2 men wounded. A few torpedoes and on without any damage.	
	21st		4 enemy snipers discovered & disposed of by our snipers. Very quiet indeed. Casualties Lieut. N.C.L. Porter wounded. O.R. 2 wounded	
	22nd			
	23rd			
	24th	6.35 p.m	Very quiet during the day. At about 6.35 p.m. enemy bombarded trenches 97 and 96 with 30 or 40 minenwerfer and many rifle grenades, followed at 7 p.m. by a bombardment of 4.5's	

WAR DIARY
or
INTELLIGENCE SUMMARY
(Erase heading not required.)

Army Form C. 2118

Place	Date	Hour	Summary of Events and Information	Remarks and references to Appendices
LE BIZET 26th June			Several men were buried in the debris, but were dug out by aid of working parties at plans. Relief, which was about to take place, was a little disorganized, and relief was not effected completed until 2.20 am 26th. D Company remained in QUINSON REDOUBT until the morning to give additional support to the Royal West Kent, in case of attack thereon — all proved quiet, and D Coy returned billets about 6 am. Morning the bombardment, our artillery retaliated for 30 minutes on the enemy trenches. They have been in retaliation against lines 98, which the previous night had opened rapid fire at a point where an enemy wiring party had been reported by our patrol, assisted by a machine gun. On a result several shots of enemy were heard, later German dead were discovered by C patrol which went out immediately afterwards. The casualties during this bombardment were 8 killed & 5 wounded and 1 man accidentally injured. Working parties continue to be found NE corner of PLOEGSTEERT WOOD	Battalion relieved. [illegible notes]

WAR DIARY
or
INTELLIGENCE SUMMARY

(Erase heading not required.)

Army Form C. 2118

Place	Date	Hour	Summary of Events and Information	Remarks and references to Appendices
Le Bizet	28th June		Commanding Officer and 4 coy commanders proceeded to reconnoitre new trenches near PLOEGSTEERT to be taken up by the battalion in a short time. No notification of party yet received.	
	29th June		Commanding Officer arrived in command, 2 company commanders and 8 platoon commanders proceeded to new sector of trenches. Total Casualties for month of June. 3 Officers wounded, O.R. 16 killed & 33 wounded.	

W.P. Bennett Lt Col

11th (S) Bn "The Queen's" (R.W.S.) Regt

Appendix II

SECRET   Copy No. 2

DEFENCE SCHEME

Reference Maps 28 and 38   1/40,000

DEFENCES The front line of the left sub-section for which the Battalion is responsible is divided up into DEFENDED LOCALITIES with GAPS in between. These GAPS are wired behind the Parados, and will be maintained as Covered Communications between DEFENDED LOCALITIES. They are to be patrolled at frequent intervals during the night and every effort made to keep enemy under the impression that they are still occupied.

DEFENDED LOCALITIES   Defended Localities are :-

      RAILWAY

      GLASGOW REDOUBT

DEFENDED POSTS (a) Defended Posts

      7 TREES REDOUBT

      RESERVE FARM

      FORT PAUL

N.B. These Posts are defended by a system of Machine Guns which cover the ground in front of the POSTS and the GAPS between the Posts.

NORMAL DISTRIBUTION OF BATTALION

Right Coy. (Left of gap "C" to left of No. 97 incl.
           (finding own support in 96 S.

Centre Coy (Left of 97 (excl) to Right of Gap "D"
           ((incl) finding own support in 97 S & Parade

Left Coy. (3 Platoons (less 1 section) GLASGOW RE-
           (DOUBT. finding own support in 102 S.
           (1 section FORT PAUL
           (1 Platoon RESERVE FARM

Local
Reserve Coy (1 Platoons PATERNOSTER ROW
            ("   7 TREES REDOUBT
            (1   "   TRENCH 98 S.

SHEET 2

DISTRIBUTION OF BATTALION

"A" Coy { Left of Gap "C" to left of 97 incl.
finding own support in 96 S.

"B" Coy { Left of 97 (excl) to right of Gap "D" (incl)
finding own support in 97 S & Parade.

"D" Coy { 3 Platoons (less 1 section) GLASGOW REDOUBT
finding own support in 102 S.
1 Section in FORT PAUL
1 Platoon in Reserve Farm

"C" Coy { 1½ Platoons PATERNOSTER ROW
1½ " 7 TREES REDOUBT
1 " 98 S.

DISTRIBUTION OF "LEWIS GUNS"

1 at Junction of Trenches 95 and 96
1 at Trench 97
1 at " 98
1 at Junction of Trenches 99 and 100 (commd. Gap D.)

If others available:-

1 at Glasgow Redoubt.
1 at 7 Trees Farm.
2 at Paternoster Row.

NORMAL DISTRIBUTION OF M.G. (Vickers) FRONT LINE.

(a) 1 gun right flank of trench 96.
1 " Centre of " 102.
1 " left flank of " 102.
─
3

SUPPORT. (b) 1 " junction of Harnians Avenue & Paternoster Row.

ACTION IN CASE OF ATTACK.

(a) Should enemy penetrate Gap C.
Fighting Sections from right Company and Support Company will at once counter attack and bomb enemy out of Gap. Reinforce Long Avenue by 1 platoon in support 97 S.

(b) Should enemy penetrate Railway locality.
Fighting Sections at the Parade will immediately counter attack moving via Essex Lane and/or Watling Street. Should this counter attack fail, the 1 platoon in Trench 97 S. will move up Essex Lane and Watling Street and counter attack. Further support if required will be forthcoming from the reserve platoons at Paternoster Row.

(c) Should enemy penetrate Gap D. The O.C."B"Coy. will at once move up 1 platoon from Bachelors Walk in support and reinforce the left flank. Counter attacks will at once be organised to drive the enemy out of gap.

SHEET 3.

ACTION IN CASE OF ATTACK.

(d). **Should the Enemy penetrate Glasgow Redoubt.**
The remainder of the Company at Reserve Farm (and Paternoster Row) will move up Suffolk Avenue and Counter Attack.

(e) **Should Enemy penetrate Gap E.**
The left of Glasgow Redoubt will be at once reinforced by 3/4 platoon from Reserve Farm. Lewis Gun No.4 being moved to that flank.
Counter attacks will be organised at once as in "C".

(f) **General.** The O.C.Coy in Battalion reserve will detail an Officer as Liason Officer, to report at Brigade Headquarters (The Convent Le Bizet).
Defended localities and defended posts will be held at all costs. The troops occupying these posts must be made to understand however much they may be outflanked, or even attacked in rear, they must hold on.
Every endeavour will be made by Commanders to keep in constant touch by Telephone, Visual Signalling, or orderly with our own troops on either flank and with those to the front or rear.
Officers Commanding Companies will satisfy themselves that all ranks understand where reserves of grenades and ammunition may be obtained, also all ranks should know their battle stations in the defended localities and the routes to them.
Tests must be carried out to ensure this. In addition every Officer and N.C.O. should know the exact routes to the defended localities on either flank.
Signallers must Test all wires every 1/4 hour.
Company Commanders must have definite plans cut and dried for defence of their localities, and this must be committed to writing.

(a) Should the Enemy penetrate into any defended locality the responsibility for ordering our Artillery to open fire on this locality will rest with the Infantry Brigade Commander concerned.

(b) In the event of the Enemy penetrating any of the Gaps between the defended localities the responsibility for ordering Artillery fire to be opened on the Gap will rest with the nearest Company Commander.

The order will be in the form of the Code Message "Q"Q"Q. G.A., G.B., G.C., etc. and will be sent to the Battery with which the Company Commander is in direct communication.
The Battery Commander will at once inform the Artillery Group Commander who will, if the Battery already warned does not cover the Gap in question, direct the Battery detailed to open fire.
The Artillery Group Commander will at once inform the C.R.A. and Divisional H.Q. of the situation.
Since it is intended that Gaps should be fired on by Artillery, Trench Mortars, M.G. & Rifles on receipt of Code Message "Q.Q.Q.G..." it must be distinctly understood that there can be no question of sending bombers to work down the Gaps from the flank of the defended locality on each side.
The action of the Bombers on the flanks of the defended localities will, in such cases be confined to preventing the hostile bombers and Infantry coming within effective throwing distance of the defended locality.
In connection with the action to be taken to meet cases (a) & (b) above, Brigade, Battalion & Company Commanders should at once organise means of rapid communication to Light Trench Mortar Batteries & M.G. in supporting points behind localities & Gaps, detailed to open fire on the Gaps.
The above in no way does away with the "S.O.S." call, but is in addition.
On the "S.O.S." Call being sent, fire is at once opened on the enemy's trenches by the artillery, and a barrage is placed between his trenches and ours.
On the call "Q Q Q G...." being sent, our Artillery at once fires into our own Gap.

SHEET 4.A.

If the enemy get into a Gap in small numbers, they are to be immediately counter-attacked by the Garrison in Front and Support Lines, and Bombing from the sides of the Gap.

If the enemy get into a Gap in large numbers, and the Company Commander on the spot considers he will be unable to turn them out without the help of the Artillery, the call "Q Q Q G..." will at once be sent.

During the time the Artillery are firing into the Gap, the men who are going to do the attack must at once get into their positions on both flanks of the Gap, and bombers ready to come up from behind.

Before the counter-attack in this case is launched, Company Commanders must make perfectly certain that the Artillery has finished its fire. This should be done by being in communication with the Battery Commander by telephone, and as soon as it is arranged between the Company Commander and the Battery Commander that the Artillery fire is to cease, and the Battery Commander reports that he has stopped, the counter-attack will be launched by some pre-arranged signal.

Artillery will only fire on a defended locality by orders from Brigade Headquarters, the reason for this being that if a part of the defended locality is rushed by the Enemy, it is not desirable to bombard and knock down the entire locality with our own Artillery, but he should be ejected by a counter-attack made by the supporting line.

Only in the event of a defended locality being completely taken, and on receipt of orders from Brigade Headquarters, will the Artillery fire into the locality.

BATTLE HEADQUARTERS. 123rd Infantry Brigade, CONVENT, LE BIZET.

     BATTALION   PATERNOSTER ROW.

ENEMY GENERAL ATTACK ALONG WHOLE FRONT.
 (a) With Gas.
  (1) Helmets to be at once put on.
  (2) Warning to be given at once to all.
  (3) All dug outs cleared.
  (4) The parapet to be manned and every gun and rifle turned on enemy.
  (5) Artillery S.O.S. call given at once.

 (b). Without Gas.
  (1) Men to take cover lying as close to the 1st line parapet as possible, with one man watching over the parapet in every 4th or 5th bay.
  (2) Men in support trenches to move as quickly as possible to adjacent AVENUES, but remain in readiness to re-man their trenches immediately on the fire being "lifted".

WORKING PARTIES. In case of sudden attack:-
 (a) All working parties from the Support & local Reserve Coy. working in the firing line, come automatically under control of the Company Commanders of the Trenches and Localities where they are working.

S.A.A.
GRENADES.
TRENCH STORES.
 The amounts allotted to:-
 1. Companies.
 2. The Battalion.

will be maintained in accordance with instructions issued to all concerned by the Brigade.

SIGNALS
TELEPHONE.
(1) Are forbidden from Battalion H.Q. to Fire Trenches, Support Trenches & Strong Points, and vice versa except in emergency, such as S.O.S. call. Runners to be substituted.
(2) To Brigade or Units in rear of Battalion H.Q. as seldom as possible. Runners used whenever possible.

CASUALTIES. To be immediately reported to M.O. and conveyed at once to Regimental AID POST with rifle and equipment. In this

SHEET 5.

connection Platoon Commanders must satisfy themselves by frequent inspection that the men carry Field Dressing always.

[signature]
Lieut. Colonel.
IIth (S) Bn. "The Queen's" Regt.

Copy No.	1.	Filed.
	2.	War Diary.
	3.	G.O.C.123rd Infy. Bde.
	4.	O.C. "A" Coy.
	5.	O.C. "B" Coy.
	6.	O.C. "C" Coy.
	7.	O.C. "D" Coy.
	8.	2nd/1/Command.
	9.	Bombing Officer.
	10.	Sniping Officer.
	11.	M.G Officer.
	12.	189th F.A. Bde.
	13.	189th F.A. Bde.
	14.	20th. D.L.I.
	15.	23rd Middlesex Regt.
	16.	10th. R.W. Kent Regt.

Rough Sketch of Trenches
Taken over by
11th Battalion "The Queen's Regt"
5.VI.16.

GERMAN LINE

NO MAN'S LAND

Gap 'D'

Gap 'E'

GLASGOW REDOUBT

FORT PAUL

SUFFOLK AVENUE

OBSERVATION FARM

PATERNOSTER ROW

DRESSING STATION

NICHOLSON AVENUE

DESSINERE FARM
Bn HQ

TREES AVENUE

POTIJZE REDOUBT

ESSEX FARM

BACHELOR'S WALK

AMEN CORNER

RAILWAY LOCALITY

HARNIAN AVENUE

Gap 'C'

To 23rd Middlesex Regt

To 1st/2nd Queen's Regt

1/5000

R.C. Smith Capt
30.6.16

DETAIL :-

A Coy - Trenches 96 & 97. NCO & 12men High Command 96.5

B Coy - Trenches 98 & 99 & Craters 97.5

C Coy - 1½ Platoons Paternoster Row.
        1½ Platoons 7 Tree Redoubt.
        1 Platoon 96.5

D Coy - 1 Platoon Reserve farm
        3 Platoons Glasgow Redoubt
        N.C.O. & 12men Fort Paul

Head Quarters. Dessinere Farm

11th Bn. THE QUEEN'S R^t. 4L July
1st July 1916 – 30th July 1916.
VOL 3

WAR DIARY
or
INTELLIGENCE SUMMARY
(Erase heading not required.)

Place	Date	Hour	Summary of Events and Information	Remarks and references to Appendices
LE BIZET	3/7/16	10pm	The Battalion relieved 10th Battalion Royal West Kent Regiment in the front line trenches. No alteration in previous disposition.	
		5pm	A reinforcement draft to 8th Battalion, Royal Fusiliers arrived and were taken on the strength of the battalion. This draft consists of 58 men. Casualties x O.R. 1 killed & 2 wounded.	
TRENCHES	4/7/16		A quiet day, only the usual sniping. In accordance with B.O.O. No. 11. the frontage occupied by the battalion was increased. Trenches 96-98 were handed over to the 23rd Middlesex, and also 4 Two Redoubt. That portion of the line occupied by the 10th Bn. R. W. Queen was taken over by A & B Companies and 2 Platoons of D Company. The disposition of the Battalion was then as under.	APP V
	5/7/16	5 am.	A Company – 1 Platoon – Lancashire Support Farm. 3 Platoons – Chicken Avenue. B Company – Trenches 108 & 1M C Company – 1 Platoon – Trench 99 1 Platoon – Bachelors Walk & part of 98S. 1½ Platoons – Patinsoli Rws. ½ Platoon – Reserve Farm & St Paul. D Company – 2 Platoons – Rasor Redoubt. Trenches 105 - 107. (see attached sketch)	

WAR DIARY
or
INTELLIGENCE SUMMARY

Army Form C. 2118

Place	Date	Hour	Summary of Events and Information	Remarks and references to Appendices
	7/7/16		Alan Fusilier Terrace was 1 Company of 10th Royal West Kent. They were in support, and came under the orders of O.C. Suffolks sector. Second Lieutenant R. Nove and 2 O.R. wounded by the premature bursting of a bomb rifle-grenade, which they were in the act of firing. Enemy's 16-pounders and snipers were more active than usual, specially during the evening. Captain W. Sharpe accidentally wounded and O.R. 1 accidentally wounded.	
	8/7/16	11.30	A quiet day. At about 11 p.m. a party of 1 officer and 20 men R. West Kent Rgt. accompanied by a party of miners with explosives, attempted a raid into German trenches from D Coy - but they were unsuccessful, the officer in charge being mortally wounded.	
	11/7/16		Nothing worthy of note.	
	12/7/16		2.1. C.A. Duesdorf slightly wounded + O.R. 2 wounded. Our artillery was unusually active. Enemy retaliated by a bombardment of trenches 99.100 ¢ 102, with minenwerfer, and aerial torpedoes and did considerable material damage. Reserve Farm was also shelled damage being done to Suffolk Avenue.	

WAR DIARY
or
INTELLIGENCE SUMMARY
(Erase heading not required.)

Army Form C. 2118

Place	Date	Hour	Summary of Events and Information	Remarks and references to Appendices
	13/7/16		Large number of shells were thrown into Glasgow Redoubt. Church 99 - but little damage was done. Capt Hogan was slightly wounded and O.R. 3 wounded. During the night 13/14th the Battalion was relieved by the 10th Royal Westkent Regiment and went back to billets, located as follows:- A Coy to Tourlin Terrace. then they were employed on working parties in Border Avenue. B Coy - Soyer Farm. C Coy - 2 Platoon - Piluent Farm. 1 Platoon - Petit Rabecq. 1 Platoon - Grand Rabecq. D Coy & Machine Gunners. Delahule Farm. Head quarters - Soyer Farm. The Battalion was employed during the week in emplacements in the supervision of the Royal Engineers.	
PLOEGSTEERT WOOD	20/7/16		Lieut L.L. Linford joined the Battalion from East Surrey Regiment.	

WAR DIARY or INTELLIGENCE SUMMARY

Army Form C. 2118

Place	Date	Hour	Summary of Events and Information	Remarks and references to Appendices
	22/7/16		3 Other Ranks wounded, while filing arrivals cart in the Bript.	
	23/7/16		5 Officers, Second Lieutenants J. V. Cooke, F. W. Tugwell, D. Maclean, C. T. Royle, A. B. Wharton arrived as reinforcement.	
	24/7/16	10 p.m.	At 10 p.m. the Battalion took over the front line trenches from 8th Bn. R.W. Kent Rgt. in the neighbourhood of Glasgow Redoubt. Considerable damage was done to parapets. Reserve Farm and Palm to Row were also subjected to shell-fire. 2 Gas cylinders were rendered leaky by the bombardment of Glasgow Redoubt, and Capt Hogan was slightly gassed in their disposal. There was much activity, too, in the neighbourhood of the Cavard. 2nd Lt Chapman, being evacuated with shell shock. Casualties. Capt. C. J. Hogan, Lieut N Chapman, wounded. O.R. killed 1, wounded 8.	
	25/7/16		Enemy showed considerable activity in the neighbourhood of the Cavard. French 110 being blown in. This was apparently the retaliation against French Mortar Battery situated near the Cavard, which had been registering during the day.	

WAR DIARY or INTELLIGENCE SUMMARY

Army Form C. 2118

Place	Date	Hour	Summary of Events and Information	Remarks and references to Appendices
	25/7/16		Our artillery was active during the day, heavy guns registering on the enemy front line. At 11pm. a violent bombardment of the enemy's defences commenced, chiefly opposite C9a4 where a company of the 20th D.L.I. made an unsuccessful raid on the enemy trenches. Great natural damage was effected. Casualties 2 Lt. Leaholm 12th Bn. Dr. Queens.	
	27/7/16		2 Lt. R. Leaholm joined from 12th Bn. Dr. Queens.	
	28/7/16		Two shells burst in our transport lines, killing 3 men, and wounding 10 others. Lce. Lieut. H. M. Todd joined from 9th Bn. R. Buffs.	

Total Casualties during the month:
Officers. Killed – Nil
Wounded – 4. Evacuated Sick – 4.

Other Ranks. Killed – 14
Wounded – 47
Died of Wounds – 5 Evacuated Sick – 21

WEEKLY STRENGTH RETURN.

	Killed.		Wounded		Missing		Evacuated Sick.		Sent to Base.		Struck off for any other cause		Officers notified as struck off.	Total Struck Off.		Reinforcements	
	Off.	O.R.	Off.	O.R.	Off.	O.R.	Off.	O.R.	Off.	O.R.	Off.	O.R.		Off.	O.R.	Off.	O.R.
Struck off Sunday July 2nd																	1
" " Monday 3rd				1												1	2
" " Tuesday 4th										1					1	1	58
" " Wednesday 5th				3				4							1	1	3
" " Thursday 6th		1		2									1		3	1	1
" " Friday 7th															2	1	1
" " Saturday 8th			1												4	1	1
Total.		1	1	5				4		1			1	1	11	-	63

*Excludes those classed "Slightly, at duty."

	Officers.	Other Ranks.
Strength last week.	30	874
Deduct Struck off.	1	11
Remaining.	29	863
Add reinforcements.	1	63
Strength this week.	30	926

DETAILS OVER.

.... Comdg.

Date July 8th 1916.

P.T.O.

D E T A I L S.

Nature	Officers.	Other Ranks.
In composite Co's. at Corps or Divisional Headquarters.		
In Convalescent Depots or Rest Camps in the Army Area.	3	20
In Field Ambulances.		
Intelligence Dept.	—	2
Officers sick (not wounded) in hospital in France.		
A.S.C. Loaders	—	2
Trench wardens.		
Road control.	—	2
Drainage Section	—	6
Tunnelling Co's., R.E.		
Divisional Salvage Coy.	1	1
Cemetary caretakers.	—	2
Examining Posts.		
Employed in Divisional Canteens or Recreation Huts.		
Any other employ which can be specified:-		
Trench Tramways	—	10
Carpenters Co R.E.	—	2
Brigade Salvage	—	2
Divisional Headquarters	—	5
TOTAL DETAILS.	4	54

Signature_____ Rank_____

Commanding_____

WEEKLY STRENGTH RETURN.

	Killed.		Wounded		Missing		Evacuated Sick.		Sent to Base.		Struck off for any other cause		Officers notified as struck off.		Total Struck off.		Reinforcements.	
	Off.	O.R.	Off.	O.R.	Off.	O.R.	Off.	O.R.	Off.	O.R.	Off.	O.R.	Off.	O.R.	Off.	O.R.	Off.	O.R.
Struck off Sunday. 9th		1											1		1	2		1
" " Monday. 10th				1												1		1
" " Tuesday. 11th																		
" " Wednesday. 12th			1	3				1							1	4	4	1
" " Thursday. 13th				1														1
" " Friday. 14th		1		1				4								2		1
" " Saturday. 15th				2														
Total.	-	2	1	9	-	-	1	5	-	-	-	-	2	-	2	16	5	5

*Excludes those classed "Slightly, at duty."

	Officers.	Other Ranks.
Strength last week.	28	926
Deduct struck off.	2	16
Remaining.	26	910
Add reinforcements.	1	5
Strength this week.	27	915

DETAILS OVER.

Lt. Col. Comdg. 1st Queens (Royal West) Regt.

Date July 15th 1916.

P. T. O.

DETAILS.

Nature.	Officers.	Other Ranks.
In composite Co's. at Corps or Divisional Headquarters.	-	5
In Convalescent Depots or Rest Camps in the Army Area.	1	20.
In Field Ambulances.		
Officers sick (not wounded) in hospital in France.		
Trench wardens.		
Road control.	-	2.
Tunnelling Co's., R.E.		
Divisional Salvage Coy.	1	1
Cemetary caretakers.	-	2
Brigade Salvage Examining Posts.	-	2
Employed in Divisional Canteens or Recreation Huts.		
Any other employ which can be specified:-		
A.S.C. Loaders.		2
Intelligence Dept		1
Drainage Section		6
Trench Tramways.	-	10.
Carpenters - C.R.E.	-	2
TOTAL DETAILS.	2	53

Signature _____ Rank _____

Commanding _____

WEEKLY STRENGTH RETURN.

	Killed.		Wounded *		Missing.		Evacuated Sick.		Sent to Base.		Struck off for any other cause		Officers notified as struck off.	Total Struck off.		Reinforcements	
	Off.	O.R.	Off.	O.R.	Off.	O.R.	Off.	O.R.	Off.	O.R.	Off.	O.R.		Off.	O.R.	Off.	O.R.
Struck off Sunday 16th																	
" Monday 17th																	
" Tuesday 18th											1				1		
" Wednesday 19th																	
" Thursday 20th								2							2		
" Friday 21st								4				5			4		1
" Saturday 22nd								1							6		
Total.								7				5			12		1

* Excludes those classed "Slightly, at duty."

	Officers.	Other Ranks.
Strength last week.	27	915
Deduct Struck off.		12
Remaining.	27	903
Add reinforcements.	1	
Strength this week.	28	903

DETAILS OVER.

.... Comdg.

Date... July 22nd 1916.

P. T. O.

DETAILS.

Nature.	Officers.	Other Ranks.
In composite Co's. at Corps or Divisional Headquarters.		
In Convalescent Depots or Rest Camps in the Army Area.	1	21
In Field Ambulances.		
Intelligence Department		
Officers sick (not wounded) in hospital in France.	—	2
A.S.C. Loaders		
Trench wardens.	—	2
Road control.	—	2
Drainage Section		
Tunnelling Co's., R.E.	—	6
Divisional Salvage Coy.	1	1
Cemetery caretakers.	—	2
Examining Posts.		
Employed in Divisional Canteens or Recreation Huts.		
Any other employ which can be specified:-		
Trench Tramways.	—	10
Carpenters 6. R.E.	—	2
Brigade Salvage	—	2
Divisional Headquarters	—	5
TOTAL DETAILS.	2	55

Signature_____ Rank_____

Commanding_____

WEEKLY STRENGTH RETURN.

	Killed.		Wounded.		Missing.		Evacuated Sick.		Sent to Base.		Struck off for any other cause		Officers notified as struck off.	Total Struck Off.		Reinforcements.	
	Off.	O.R.	Off.	O.R.	Off.	O.R.	Off.	O.R.	Off.	O.R.	Off.	O.R.		Off.	O.R.	Off.	O.R.
Struck off Sunday 23rd	-	3	-	-	-	-	-	1	-	-	-	-		-	4	-	-
" " Monday 24th	-	-	-	-	-	4	-	-	-	-	-	-		-	-	-	1
" " Tuesday 25th	-	-	-	1	-	-	-	-	-	-	-	-		-	-	1	5
" " Wednesday 26th	1	-	-	2	-	5	-	1	-	-	-	-		1	4	-	1
" " Thursday 27th	-	3	-	-	-	4	-	-	-	-	-	1		-	3	-	1
" " Friday 28th	-	-	1	-	-	2	-	1	-	-	-	-		1	9	1	-
" " Saturday 29th	-	1	-	-	-	-	-	1	-	-	-	-		-	4	-	1
" "	-	-	-	-	-	-	-	-	-	-	-	-		1	3	-	-
Total.	1	7	3	15	-	-	-	4	-	-	-	1		3	27	7	-

* Excludes those classed "Slightly, at duty."

	Officers.	Other Ranks.
Strength last week.	28	903
Deduct Struck off.	3	27
Remaining.	25	876
Add reinforcements.	7	1
Strength this week.	32	877

DETAILS OVER.

Comdg. 11th (S) Bn The Queens Regt

Date 29th July 1916.

P.T.O.

DETAILS.

Nature.	Officers.	Other Ranks.
In composite Co's. at Corps or Divisional Headquarters.		
In Convalescent Depots or Rest Camps in the Army Area.	3	20.
In Field Ambulances.		
Intelligence Department		
Officers sick (not wounded) in hospital in France.	—	2.
A.S.C. Loaders		2
Trench wardens.	—	2.
Road control.	—	2.
Drainage Section		
Tunnelling Co's., R.E.	—	6
Divisional Salvage Coy.	1	1.
Cemetary caretakers.	—	2
Examining Posts.		
Employed in Divisional Canteens or Recreation Huts.		
Any other employ which can be specified:-		
Trench Tramways	—	10
Carpenters, &c R.E.	—	2
Brigade Salvage	—	2.
Divisional Headquarters	—	5.
TOTAL DETAILS.	4.	54

Signature _____ Rank

Commanding

Rough Sketch of Trenches
taken over
from 10th Bn "The Queens" on July 6th 1916

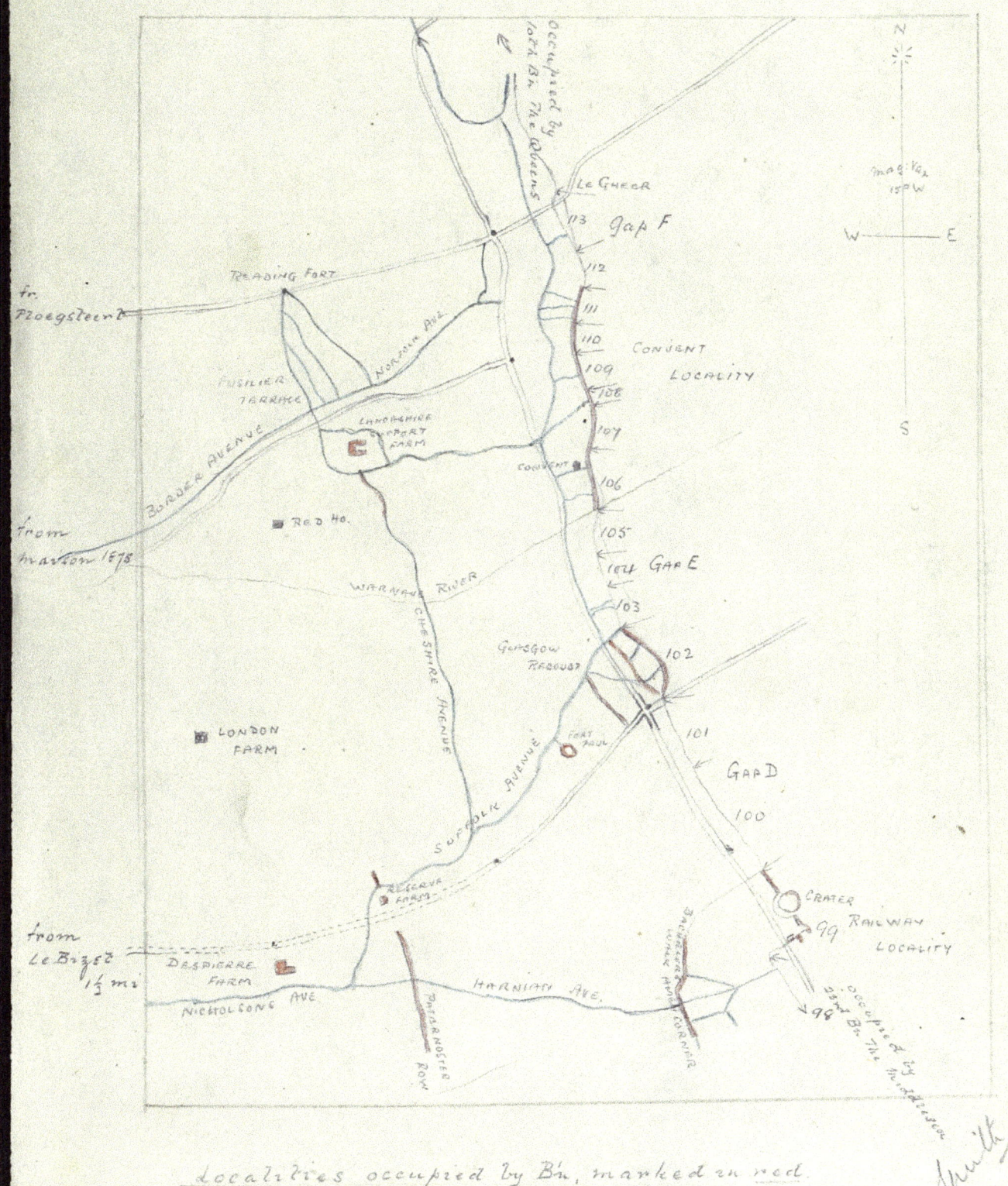

Localities occupied by Bn. marked in red.

DISPOSITIONS
'A' Coy — 1 Platoon Lancashire Support Farm
        — 3 Platoons Cheshire Avenue
'B' Coy — Trenches 106–111
'C' Coy — 1 Platoon Trench 99
        — 1 Platoon Bachelors Walk and 98
        — 1½ Platoons Paternoster Row
        — ½ Platoon Rosecoe Farm and Fort Paul
'D' Coy — 2 Platoons Glasgow Redoubt
        — 2 Platoons Trenches 106 and 107

R C Smith Capt
29/VII/16

ORIGINAL

WAR DIARY or **INTELLIGENCE SUMMARY**

11TH BN "THE QUEEN'S" REGT. Army Form C. 2118

JULY 30TH - AUGUST 29TH 1916.

VOL 4

Place	Date	Hour	Summary of Events and Information	Remarks and references to Appendices
TRENCHES	1/8/16		The Battalion was relieved by the 10th Bn. R.W. Kent Regiment and went back into the actual billets in LE BIZET, where after a good days rest, working parties were continued executing important work in PLOEGSTEERT WOOD, under supervision of Royal Engineers.	
LE BIZET	9/8/16		From 9 a.m. till 2.40 p.m. the enemy shelled the battery of artillery located some 150 yards WEST of LE BIZET, with 5.9" shells. The second shell fall hit one of D Coy' billets, killing 2 men and wounding 5. About an hour later 2 shells in rapid succession hit the the same down Sun billet, and killed 8 and wounded 15 Chms Gunners. That evening Brigade Order No 20 was received, arranged for 1 Company to be billeted in GRANDE RABEQUE, 1 Company in PETITE RABEQUE, the 3rd to remain in cellars in LE BIZET. (B Company was back in STEENWERCK after this time). The billets were therefor allted to A Coy in LE BIZET, B Coy in laundry, French LE BIZET, C Coy GRANDE RABEQUE and D Coy PETITE RABEQUE.	

WAR DIARY
or
INTELLIGENCE SUMMARY

(Erase heading not required.)

Army Form C. 2118

Instructions regarding War Diaries and Intelligence Summaries are contained in F. S. Regs., Part II. and the Staff Manual respectively. Title Pages will be prepared in manuscript.

Place	Date	Hour	Summary of Events and Information	Remarks and references to Appendices
LE BIZET	12/8		The battalion relieved the 10th Royal Welsh Regiment in the trenches	
	17/8		The battalion was relieved by 10th Bn. NORTHUMBERLAND FUSILIERS, and marched by platoons to billets in STEENWERCK, for the night	
	18/8		The battalion proceeded by march route to billets at FONTAINE HOUCK where it was billeted in 5 farm houses. Thence the time was spent in route marches and athletics to make the men fit after their tour of the trenches.	
	24/8		Battalion proceeded by train from BAILLEUL STATION to LONGPRÉ, arriving there at 10 a.m. Thence by march route to billets in BUSSUS-BUSSUEL. The next day vigorous training in the attack was commenced. Special attention being paid to the inculcation of the offensive spirit.	
			TOTAL CASUALTIES O.R. 12 killed 27 wounded	

at 2.30 a.m.

11th (S) Bn "The Queen's" Regt.

WEEKLY STRENGTH RETURN

	Killed		Wounded		Missing		Evacuated Sick		Sent to Base		Struck off for any other cause		Officers rank and as struck off		Total		Reinforcements	
	Off	O.R	Off	O.R	Off	O.R	Off	O.R	Off	O.R	Off	O.R	Off	O.R	Off	O.R	Off	O.R
Struck off Sunday July 30th	-	-	-	10	-	-	-	1	-	-	-	-	-	-	1	18	1	1
" " Monday 31st	-	3	-	1	-	-	-	8	-	-	-	-	-	1	1	4	1	1
" " Tuesday Aug 1st	-	1	-	1	-	-	-	1	-	-	-	1	-	1	1	1	1	1
" " Wednesday 2nd	-	1	-	1	-	-	-	8	-	-	1	1	1	1	1	4	1	1
" " Thursday 3rd	-	-	-	1	-	-	-	1	-	-	-	1	-	1	1	1	1	1
" " Friday 4th	-	1	-	1	-	-	-	-	-	-	-	-	-	-	1	1	1	-
" " Saturday 5th	-	-	-	-	-	-	-	5	-	-	-	-	-	-	1	5	1	1
TOTALS	-	5	-	10	-	-	-	11	-	-	1	1	1	1	1	27	-	3

Excludes those classed "Slightly at Duty"

	Officers	Other Ranks
Strength last week	32	877
Struck off	1	27
Remaining	31	850
Reinforcements	-	3
Strength this week	31	853

DETAILS OVER

Mahull - Capt. & A/Lieut Colonel
Commanding 11th (S) Bn "The Queen's" Regt.

Date

DETAILS

Nature of	Officers	Other Ran.
	1	1
Dept		
		1
		2
Divisional Headquarters		5

Total	Officers	Other Ran.

Weekly Strength Return

	Killed		Wounded*		Missing		Evacuated sick		Sent to Base		Struck off any other cause		Officers not officially struck off	Total struck off		Reinforcements
	Off	OR	Off	OR	Off	OR	Off	OR	Off	OR	Off	OR		Officers	OR	
Struck off Sunday 6th	–	–	–	–	–	–	–	–	–	–	–	–	–	–	–	–
" " Monday 7th	–	–	–	–	–	–	–	–	–	–	–	–	–	–	–	1
" " Tuesday 8th	–	–	–	–	–	–	–	–	–	–	–	–	–	–	–	–
" " Wednesday 9th	–	–	–	–	–	–	–	–	–	–	–	–	–	–	–	1
" " Thursday 10th	–	8	–	20	–	–	–	–	–	–	–	–	–	–	28	1
" " Friday 11th	–	–	–	1	–	–	–	3	–	–	–	–	–	–	4	–
" " Saturday 12th	–	–	–	–	–	–	–	–	–	–	–	–	1	–	–	2
Total	–	8	–	21	–	–	–	3	–	–	–	–	1	–	32	4

* excludes those "slightly at duty"

	Officers	Other Ranks
Strength Last week	37	853
Total struck off	–	32
Remaining	37	821
Add reinforcements	–	4
Strength this week	37	825

DETAILS OVER

R Shirth
Capt & Lt Col. Comg 11th (S) Bn. The Queens (Royal) Regt.

Date 12th August 1916.

P.T.O

DETAILS

Nature of	Officers	Other Rks
In Divisional Rest / F.A.	1	21
Road Control	—	2
Divisional Salvage Corps	1	1
Cemetery Crouchers	—	2
A.S.C. Loaders	—	2
Intelligence Dept	—	2
Drainage Section	—	7
Trench Tramways	—	10
Carpenters C.R.E.	—	2
Brigade Salvage	—	2
Divisional Headquarters	—	5
Totals	2	56

Weekly Casualty Return

	Killed		Wounded		Missing		Evacuated sick		Wounded sent to Base		Struck off and other cases		Officers notifications struck off	Total struck off		Reinforcements	
	Off	OR	Off	OR	Off	OR	Off	OR	Off	OR	Off	OR	Off	Officers	OR	Off	OR
Sunday 13th	-	-	-	-	-	-	-	-	-	-	-	-	-	-	-	-	-
Monday 14th	-	-	-	1	-	-	-	-	-	-	-	-	-	-	1	-	-
Tuesday 15th	-	-	-	1	-	-	-	-	-	-	-	-	1	1	1	-	1
Wednesday 16th	-	-	-	4	-	-	-	4	-	-	-	-	-	-	4	-	-
Thursday 17th	-	-	-	-	-	-	-	-	-	-	-	-	-	-	-	-	-
Friday 18th	-	-	-	-	-	-	-	-	-	-	-	-	-	-	-	-	-
Saturday 19th	-	-	-	1	-	-	-	-	-	-	-	-	-	-	1	-	1
Total	-	-	-	6	-	-	-	4	-	-	-	-	1	1	10	-	1

* Excludes those "slightly at duty"

	Officers	Other Ranks
Strength last week	31	823
Deduct struck off	1	10
Remaining	30	813
Add reinforcements	-	1
Strength this week	30	814

DETAILS OVER

P.T.O.

R. Smith, Capt. for Lieut. Comd. 11th (S) Bn. The Queens (Roy.) Regt.

Date 19th August 1916.

Nature of	Officers	OR
In Divisional Rest & F.A.	—	24
Road Control	—	2
Divisional Salvage Coy	1	1
Cemetery Caretakers	—	—
A.S.C. Loaders	—	2
Intelligence Department	—	1
Drainage Section (Returned to Unit)	—	1
French Tramways " " "	—	1
Carpenters C.R.E.	—	1
Brigade Salvage	—	2
Divisional Headquarters	—	5
Total	1	38

Weekly Killed & Wounded

	Killed	Wounded*	Missing	Estimated Sick	Admitted to Sick	Struck off on other cause	Officers notifications struck off	Total struck off	Reinforcement
					Off. O.R.	Off. O.R.	Off.	Off. O.R.	Off. O.R.
August Sunday 20									
" Monday 21									1
" Tuesday 22									5
" Wednesday 23									
" Thursday 24									
" Friday 25									
" Saturday 26							1	1	
Total							1	1	6

* Excludes those "slightly at duty"

	Officers	Other Ranks
Strength last week	30	816
Deduct struck off	1	—
Remaining	29	816
Add reinforcements	—	6
Strength this week	29	822

DETAILS OVER

J. B. Burlowly, Major
Comg. 11/4 (S) Bn. The Queens (Royal) Regt.

Date: 26th August 1916.

P.T.O.

Nature of Work	Officers	O.R.
In Divisional Rest & F.A.	—	31
Road Control	—	2
Divisional Salvage Coy.	1	1
Cemetery Caretakers	—	—
A.S.C. Loaders	—	2
Intelligence Department	—	1
Drainage Section (Returned to Unit)	—	—
Trench Tramways	—	—
Brigade Salvage	—	3
Divisional Headquarters	—	5
Brigade Office	—	2

Original

Army Form C. 2118

11TH Bn THE QUEENS 1st Sept. 1916 - 30th Sept 1916

VOL 5

WAR DIARY
or
INTELLIGENCE SUMMARY
(Erase heading not required.)

Instructions regarding War Diaries and Intelligence Summaries are contained in F.S. Regs., Part II. and the Staff Manual respectively. Title Pages will be prepared in manuscript.

Place	Date	Hour	Summary of Events and Information	Remarks and references to Appendices
Bussus-Bussuel	1st to 5th		Battalion remained and billets. Usual training carried on. Special attention being paid to "The Attack".	
	6th		The Transport proceeded to MÉAULTE via AMIENS	
	7th		The battalion left BUSSUS for MÉAULTE by Cattle train leaving LONGPRÉ at 3 p.m. Arrived at MÉRICOURT at 5 p.m. and bivouacked near MÉAULTE at 11.30 p.m.	
	8th		LT. COL. H.B. BURNABY, Commanding the battalion, was killed whilst reconnoitring the front line trenches near DEVILLE WOOD with the 4 company commanders. MAJ WARDEN assumed Command of the battalion.	
	9th		Battalion moved to FRICOURT CAMP.	
	10th	9pm	Battalion left camp to take over trenches occupied by 9th Battn. The Kings Rgt. The 1st Bn New Zealand Rifle Brigade were on the left and 23rd Middlesex Rgt on the right. Dispositions of company were as follows:-	Appendix 1
			Head Quarters - CARLTON TRENCH A COY - In rear of B COY B COY - TEA LANE - right on FLEES ROAD C COY - TEA TRENCH D COY - ORCHARD TRENCH	

WAR DIARY or INTELLIGENCE SUMMARY

Army Form C. 2118

Place	Date	Hour	Summary of Events and Information	Remarks and references to Appendices
DELVILLE WOOD	11th	5 a.m.	Relief reported complete. Enemy bombarded the trenches, intermittently, all day with high explosives. The trenches were considerably damaged, and the men were employed in digging and mending the same most of the day. Delville Wood was also subjected to bombardment at frequent intervals. Assembly trenches for troops to be employed in attack on Ferms on 15th Sept were dug in front of the wood.	
	13th	1 a.m.	The battalion was relieved by the 20th Durham Light Infantry, the positions of companies then being :- Head-Quarters - CARLTON TRENCH A Coy - YORK TRENCH B Coy - CARLTON TRENCH C Coy - SAVOY TRENCH D - ORCHARD TRENCH	APPENDIX I
		9 p.m.	The battalion was relieved by the 18th K.R.R. and marched into MONTAUBAN ALLEY. The total casualties during the tour of duty near DELVILLE WOOD were: killed O.Rs 5; Wounded Officers 4, O.R. 44	

Army Form C. 2118

WAR DIARY or INTELLIGENCE SUMMARY
(Erase heading not required.)

Place	Date	Hour	Summary of Events and Information	Remarks and references to Appendices
MONTAUBAN ALLEY	14th	9.30 a.m.	Brigade Order No. 31 was received. This dealt with the part the 123rd Brigade was to play in the attack by the 41st Division on FLERS, Sept. 15th. The brigade being held in reserve, and the battalion the reserve battalion of the brigade.	APP. II
	15th	12.30 a.m.	Major OTTER. 20th Norfolk Regiment, attached to 20th Bn. Royal Fusiliers arrived to take over command of the battalion.	
		11.30 a.m.	The battalion moved from MONTAUBAN ALLEY to CHECK TRENCH, and at 2.30 p.m. moved on to CARLTON TRENCH.	
		7.30 p.m.	Orders were issued verbally to Commanding Officer for the battalion to move forward to consolidate the position round FLERS, which had been won by 120th Brigade during the day. The responsibility for the defence of FLERS being passed to Major OTTER.	
		11.25 p.m.	The battalion moved via MILK ALLEY and was led East of FLERS to a position both N.E. of the village as shown on accompanying sketch when it proceeded to dig itself in. This was completed by dawn. Communication was at once established with the 10th Durham Light Infantry on the right, and with the aid of a company of Royal Fusiliers left by orders of patrols	MAP II APP. II

WAR DIARY
or
INTELLIGENCE SUMMARY

(Erase heading not required.)

Army Form C. 2118

Instructions regarding War Diaries and Intelligence Summaries are contained in F.S. Regs., Part II. and the Staff Manual respectively. Title Pages will be prepared in manuscript.

Place	Date	Hour	Summary of Events and Information	Remarks and references to Appendices
FLERS	15th		23rd Middlesex were completing the right of the Divisional Front after relieving points Box & Cox. Machine guns were established in the Flanders Road 500 yards East of the village.	
	16th	8 a.m.	Enemy began to shell FLERS very heavily with guns of all Calibres. Also the road leading from FLERS to GUEUDECOURT, near Box & Cox and FLEA TRENCH. See Intelligence Report.	
	17th		See Intelligence Report. During the night the Battalion was relieved by 1/7th Du. Kings Regt. and marched back to camp at MÉAULTE.	
	18th		Reinforcements of 140 men were taken into strength of the battalion. The casualties during operations of 15th, 16th, 17th were	
			Killed O.R. 4	
			Wounded Officers 3	
			O.R. 40	
			During the next few days, the training of the battalion was continued, & also reorganisation of companies	

WAR DIARY or INTELLIGENCE SUMMARY

Army Form C. 2118

Place	Date	Hour	Summary of Events and Information	Remarks and references to Appendices
	27th	6 p.m.	The battalion moved to bivouac near MONTAU BAN.	
	28th	1 p.m.	The battalion moved to CARLTON TRENCH, where in accordance with B.O. No 32	
		7.30 p.m.	Relieved King's Own Regiment in trenches in neighbourhood of FACTORY CORNER. A Coy in Reserve near FACTORY CORNER. B. Coy in support in GIRD TRENCH. C & D Coys in GIRD SUPPORT.	See MAP II APP II
	29th		Enemy held SHELLED FIELD, and all trenches held by the Battalion all day with heavy artillery.	Reinforced in evening. Enemy Consolidated APP II
		7 p.m.	During the night C & D Coys advanced some 100 yards and consolidated the ground. A party of Engineers put out wire in front.	
	30th	2 p.m.	Intense heavy shelling took place. C & D Coys were relieved by 2 Companies 20th Durham Light Infantry but owing to heavy shelling completion of relief was postponed until	
		6.30 p.m.	after dark, when 2 more coys of 20th D.L.I. relieved A & B Coys. The battalion was then disposed of as under:— B Coy – SMOKE TRENCH A Coy – SMOKE SUPPORT C Coy ⎫ Sunken Road, 500 yds D. ⎭ East of FLERS H.Q. Included	See APP III

The Casualties for the 3 days 29th 30th Sept. were

Killed O.R. 17
Wounded Officers 1
          O.R. 73
Missing O.R. 2

R. Otter Lt.Col.
Cmdg 11th Bn The Queens Regt.

Weekly Strength Return

	Killed		Wounded Missing		Accidental Sick		Sent to Base		Known previously Wounded		Prisoners Since of		Total Since of		Reinforcements	
	Off	OR	Off	OR	Off	OR	Off	OR	Off	OR	Off	OR	Off	OR	Off	OR
Since Sunday 26																1
Monday 27										1				1		1
Tuesday 28																
Wednesday 29																7
Thursday 30																
Friday 1																
Saturday 2									1					1		9
													1	3		

† Considers there slightly at duty"
‡ 2 OR was transferred to R.F.C.

DETAILS OVER

	Officers	Other Ranks
Strength last week	39	832
Less casualties of	1	2
Reinforcements	28	—
Less transfers	—	4
Strength this week	28	829

2nd September 1916
J.W.B. Burney Lt. Col.
11th Bn "The Queen's" Regt.

Nature of Work	Officers	O.R.
In Divisional Rest + F.A.		34
Road Control		2
Divisional Salvage Coy	1	1
A.S.C. Loaders		2
Intelligence Dept		1
Brigade Salvage		2
Divisional Headquarters		5
Base (underage)		10
123rd Brigade		8
123rd T.M. Battery	1	23
123rd M.G. Coy		11
Battalion Stormen		1
	2	100

11TH (S) BN THE QUEENS (R.W.S.) Regt

WEEKLY STRENGTH RETURN

	Killed		Wounded +		Missing		Evacuated Sick		Sent to Base		Struck off other purposes		Officers notified struck off		TOTAL Struck off		Reinforcements	
	Off.	O.R.	Off.	O.R.	Off.	O.R.	Off.	O.R.	Off.	O.R.	Off.	O.R.	Off.	O.R.	Off.	O.R.	Off.	O.R.
SUNDAY 3rd																		1
MONDAY 4th										12								
TUESDAY 5th																		
WEDNESDAY 6th																		
THURSDAY 7th																		
FRIDAY 8th		1																
SATURDAY 9th ⊕		1								12								1

+ Excludes those "slightly at duty"

DETAILS OVER.

	Strength last week	Deduct struck off	Remaining	Add reinforcements	Strength this week
OFFICERS.	28		27		27
O.R.	829		817		818

9th September 1916
⊕ Lt Col. H.R. Burnaby D.S.O.

Alfred Taylor Lt Col.
Commanding 11th Bn The Queens R.W.S. Regt.

Nature of Work	Officers	O.R.
Divisional Rest & F.A.		37
Road Control		3
Divisional Salvage Coy	1	1
A.S.C. Loaders		2
Intelligence Dept		1
Brigade Salvage		2
Divisional Headquarters		5
Base (underage)		12
125th Brigade		8
" T.M. Battery	1	23
" M.G. Coy		11
Battalion Storeman		1
	2	106

11th (S) Bn THE QUEENS (R.W.S.) Regt

WEEKLY STRENGTH RETURN

	Killed		Wounded		Missing		Evacuated Sick		Sent to Base		Struck off other purposes		Officers notified Struck off		TOTAL Struck off		Reinforcements	
	Off	O.R.	Off	O.R.	Off	O.R.	Off	O.R.	Off	O.R.	Off	O.R.	Off	O.R.	Off	O.R.	Off	O.R.
SUNDAY 10	—	—	—	—	—	—	—	—	—	—	—	—	—	—	—	—	—	—
MONDAY 11	—	—	2	6	—	—	—	—	—	—	—	—	—	—	2	6	5	—
TUESDAY 12	—	1	1	11	—	—	—	—	—	—	—	—	—	—	1	12	—	—
WEDNESDAY 13	—	—	—	—	—	—	—	—	—	—	—	—	—	—	—	—	—	60
THURSDAY 14	—	—	—	—	—	—	—	—	—	—	—	—	—	—	—	—	—	—
FRIDAY 15	—	4	4	40	—	—	—	—	—	—	—	—	—	—	4	44	—	—
SATURDAY 16	—	5	—	—	—	—	—	—	—	—	—	—	—	—	1	62	5	60
	—	5	7	57											7			

+ Excludes those last week
※ Excludes those "slightly at duty"

DETAILS OVER.

	OFFICERS	O.R.
Strength last week	27	818
Deduct Struck off	7	62
Remaining	20	756
Add Reinforcements	5	60
Strength this week	25	816

16th September 1916

R. Whitelaw Lt Col.
Commdg 11th Bn "The Queens R.W.S. Regt"

11TH (S) BN THE QUEENS (R.W.S.) REGT

WEEKLY STRENGTH RETURN

	Killed		Wounded †		Missing		Evacuated Sick		Sent to Base		Struck off other Purposes		Officers notified Struck off		TOTAL Struck off		Reinforcements	
	Off.	O.R.	Off.	O.R.	Off.	O.R.	Off.	O.R.	Off.	O.R.	Off.	O.R.	Off.	O.R.	Off.	O.R.	Off.	O.R.
SUNDAY 17	—	—	5	36	—	—	—	—	—	—	—	—	—	—	5	36	6	80
MONDAY 18																		10
TUESDAY 19																		18
WEDNESDAY 20																		
THURSDAY 21																		
FRIDAY 22																		
SATURDAY 23	—	—	5	36	—	—	—	—	—	—	—	—	—	—	5	36	6	108

† Excludes those "slightly at duty"

DETAILS OVER.

	OFFICERS	O.R.
Strength last week	25	816
Deduct Struck off	5	36
Reinforcements	20	780
Add Reinforcements this week	6	108
Strength	26	888

13th September 1916

Allenby Lt. Col.
Commrdg. 11th Bn The Queens R.W.S. Regt.

Nature of Work	Officers	O.R.
Divisional Rest & F.A.		33
" Salvage	1	1
Road Control		3
A.S.C. Loaders		2
Intelligence Dept		1
Brigade Salvage		2
Divisional Headquarters		5
Base (underage)		12
123rd Brigade		8
" T.M. Battery	1	23
" M.G Coy		11
Batt.n Storeman		1
	2	102

11TH (S) BN THE QUEEN'S (R.W.S.) REGT

WEEKLY STRENGTH RETURN

	Killed		Wounded +		Missing		Evacuated Sick		Sent to Base		Struck off other purposes		Officers notified/left Struck off		TOTAL Struck off		Reinforcements	
	Off	O.R.	Off	O.R.	Off	O.R.	Off	O.R.	Off	O.R.	Off	O.R.	Off	O.R.	Off	O.R.	Off	O.R.
SUNDAY 24	-	1	-	-	-	-	-	-	-	-	-	-	-	-	-	1	-	1
MONDAY 25	-	-	-	-	-	-	-	-	-	-	-	-	-	-	-	-	-	-
TUESDAY 26	-	-	-	-	-	-	-	-	-	-	-	-	-	-	-	-	-	-
WEDNESDAY 27	-	-	-	-	-	-	-	-	-	-	-	-	-	-	-	-	-	4
THURSDAY 28	-	-	-	-	-	-	-	-	-	-	-	-	-	-	-	-	-	1
FRIDAY 29	-	-	-	-	-	-	-	-	-	-	-	-	-	-	-	-	-	-
SATURDAY 30	-	1	-	-	-	-	-	-	-	-	-	-	-	-	-	1	-	5

+ Excludes those "slightly at duty"

DETAILS OVER

	OFFICERS	O.R.
Strength last week	26	858
Deduct Struck off	-	1
Remaining	26	857
Add Reinforcements	-	5
Strength this week	26	862

30th September 1916

A. Clarke Kennedy Lt Col.
Commdg. 11th Bn The Queen's R.W.S. Regt.

Nature of Work	Officers	O.R.
Divisional Rest & T.A.		36
Road Control		3
Divisional Salvage	1	1
A.S.C. Loaders		2
Intelligence Dept		1
Brigade Salvage		2
Divl Headquarters		5
Base (underage)		12
123rd Brigade		8
" T.M. Battery	1	23
" M.G. Coy.		11
Batt Storeman (Steenwerck)		1
	2	105

App. II

SECRET.   Copy No....9........

123rd INFANTRY BRIGADE ORDER No.31.

Reference Maps:-
Special Map attached "A".
Trench Maps already issued.
LONGUEVAL 57c. S.W. 3.

INFORMATION. 1. The 41st Division, in co-operation with other Divisions of the XV Corps is to attack and capture the enemy system of defences on its front on the 15th September (Z day). Other troops of the 4th Army and French are co-operating.

The attack will be pushed home with the utmost vigour all along the line until the most distant objectives have been reached. For the last 2½ months we have been gradually wearing down the enemy. His moral is shaken, he has few, if any, fresh Reserves available, and there is every probability that a combined determined effort will result in a decisive victory.

The rôle of the 41st Division is to capture the enemy's defences (including FLERS) up to and including the line Pt. N 20.d.5.0. (exclusive) - N.20.c.3.3. - Road Junction N.25 b.0.6.

The 41st Division will be in the centre, with the 14th Division on its right and the New Zealand Division on its left.

DISPOSITIONS AND STAGES OF ATTACK 2. The 124th and 122nd Infantry Brigades will be in the front line (124th Infantry Brigade on the right). The 123rd Infantry Brigade will be in Divisional Reserve.

Each Infantry Brigade will have 1 Section R.E. from their affiliated Field Coys. R.E. attached.

The operations are divided into four (4) stages, and each line will be captured successively:-

1st Objective (Green Line).

The enemy's trenches 800 yards South of FLERS (SWITCH LINE), from junction with COCOA LANE (excl.) to junction with COFFEE LANE S.3.c.2.7. (excl).
No Halt will be made in TEA SUPPORT TRENCH.

2nd. Objective (Brown Line).

Enemy's trenches running S.E., on the S.W. and S. sides of FLERS (FLERS LINE) from T 1.b.1.2. to M 36.d.3.4.

3rd Objective (Blue Line).

The village of FLERS and the line, Cross Roads N.31.b.4.0. - N. edge of FLERS to Road Junction N.31.a.2.5. (excl.)

4th Objective (Red Line).

Establish line N.20.d.5.0. (excl) - N.20.c.3.6. - Road Junction N.25.b.0.6. (Track excl.).

The objectives in several cases consist of a double line of trenches. Where this is the case the troops will be given the trench furthest away from us as their Objective, steps being taken to deal adequately with the intermediate trench.

2.

ASSEMBLY. 3. The 123rd Infantry Brigade will be in position with regiments in their assembly trenches by 11 p.m. 14th inst. (vide Appendix "A" and Map "B" attached).

1 Officer and 4 N.C.O's per Coy. will reconnoitre the route to the trenches, and the trenches themselves during the afternoon of the 14th inst.

Tape can be obtained from Brigade Headquarters if required, to tape out the end limits of the trenches. The Troops at present occupying these trenches will be clear by 9 p.m. 14th inst. of the area S. of York Trench.

S.A.A., Grenades, flares &c. as per Appendix "B" will be brought to Brigade Headquarters on the afternoon of the 14th inst., from where units will draw them on receiving instructions to do so.

APPROACH AVENUES. 4. Allotted to 123rd Infantry Brigade:- FLARE LANE. MILK LANE.

DIVIDING LINES. 5. (a) Dividing Line between the Right of 124th Infantry Brigade and the Left Brigade 14th Division will be:-
The line Pt. S.22.c.9.2. - S.17.d.9.3. - thence COCOA LANE to its junction with SWITCH LINE - T.1.d.0.2. (incl. to 14th Division) - Road Junction T.1.b.1.2. (incl. to 14th Divn.) -Road Junction N.31.b.4.0. (incl. to 41st Divn.) - Strong Pt.N.31.b.5.2. (incl. to 41st Divn.) - Road Junction N.26.c.4.4. (incl. to 14th Divn.) - Road Junction N.26.a.9.1. (incl. to 14th Divn.) - Road Junction N.21.c.0.6. (incl. to 14th Divn.)

(b) Dividing Line between 124th Infantry Brigade and 122nd Infantry Brigade - S.22.c.8.6. to Cross Roads S.17.b.3.4. inclusive of FLARE LANE - thence via LONGUEVAL - FLERS Road to its junction at S.3.b.9.3. - T.1.a.4.8. - N.31.c.85.45.- N.31.b.15.15. - N.31 b.2.6. thence along track to N.30.c.4.4. (all incl. to 124th Inf. Bde.)

(c) Dividing Line between 122nd Infantry Brigade and the Right Brigade New Zealand Division:-

S.21.d.8.7. - Junction of Tracks at S.16.d.1.6. - thence to S.11.c.0.4. - S.11.d.0.8. - Junction of PEACH TRENCH and TEA TRENCH (incl. to 41st Divn.) COFFEE LANE (incl. to N.Z. Divn.) - N.36.d.3.3. - Road Junction at N.36.b.5.0. (incl. to N.Z. Divn). - Cross Roads at N.31.a.2.5. (incl. to N.Z. Divn.) - N.25.b.0.3. (Track incl. to N.Z. Divn.).

DIRECTING FLANK. 6. The right of the 122nd Infantry Brigade will direct. General direction of attack 28° True Bearing.

ARTILLERY. 7. The Artillery bombardment of the enemy's defensive system commenced on the 12th inst.

The Divisional Artillery will form creeping barrages as shown in APPENDIX C. The attacking troops will advance immediately behind these barrages, and not more than 50 yards distance between waves.

HOUR OF ASSAULT. 8. At "ZERO" hour which will be notified later the 122nd and 124th Infantry Brigades advance. The 123rd Infantry Brigade will not move from its position of assembly until orders are received from Brigade Headquarters.

When orders are received to advance, units will advance in artillery formations of platoons. During the advance LONGUEVAL must be avoided as far as possible. Troops that have moved off their line of direction to pass LONGUEVAL must correct their direction as soon as they are clear of the village.

R.E. 9. 1 Section 233rd Field Coy. R.E. will be attached to the 10th Royal West Kent Regt. and will move with them.

This section will report at Brigade Headquarters at POMMIERS REDOUBT, at 8 p.m. 14th inst.

TANKS.   10. TEN tanks, Heavy Section M.G. Corps will co-operate in the attack.

The role of these tanks is to destryo the Hostile Machine Guns and Strong Points, and clear the way for the Infantry. They will usually precede the Infantry.

Infantry must follow behind the tanks, and should any strong point succeed in holding up the Infantry they will call for a tank to assist them. The Signal will be for "Enemy in Sight" with the Rifle.

Each tank has an escort of 1 N.C.O. and 10 men, and should the tanks get in rear of the Infantry or for any reason be obliged to withdraw across ground over which Infantry has passed, the escort will remove any wounded which happen to lie in the path of the tank. The escort will also protect the tank from close assault.

Should the tanks become out of action at any time and be unable to advance, (especially on the advance from FLERS TRENCH to attack the village when the tanks are supposed to precede the Infantry by 15 minutes) the Infantry are on no account to wait for them, but will advance at the hour arranged for the tanks in order that they may derive the benefit of the Artillery barrage. This necessary action must be decided on by the Officers in Command of troops on the spot.

As soon as the final objective has been established the tanks will be withdrawn to a position South of LONGUEVAL to replenish.

The following signals will be used from tanks to Infantry and aircraft:-

FLAG SIGNALS.

RED FLAG.   =   OUT OF ACTION.
GREEN FLAG.   =   AM ON OBJECTIVE.
Other flags are inter-tank signals.

LAMP SIGNALS.

Series of "T's" = OUT OF ACTION.
Series of "H's" = AM ON OBJECTIVE

Infantry must not wait for tanks that get behind time table.

OBJECTIVES AND 11. The successive objectives are given in para. 2.
RATE OF   The advance will be carried out in accordance with the
ADVANCE.   attached time table.

CLEARING UP.   12. Each Company will detail a "Mopping up" party of
               1 Officer and 20 men. They will be used if required.
               Each man of the "Mopping up" parties will carry one "P" Grenade.

CONSOLIDATION. 13. Each objective will be consolidated as soon as possible after its capture, and made secure against counter attack.

COMMUNICATION 14. Each Battalion will tell off a special party
TRENCHES.   consisting of 1 Officer and 50 Other Ranks to dig
                   communication between our front line and the German line in
                   case they are required. This party should be detailed from
                   the rear Company of each Battalion.

STRONG POINTS. 15. The 124th Infantry Brigade will construct Strong
               Points at the following places:-
               Junction of Trenches T.7.a.2.6.
               S.6.d.72.67.
               T.1.c.95.25.
               T.1.a.2.5.
               N.31.b.19.50.
               N.31.b.5.3.
               N.26.a.5.8.

4.

122nd Infantry Brigade will construct Strong Points as below:-

    S.6.d.0.5.
    S.6.c.75.55.
    S.6.b.80.85.
    T.1.a.4.9.
    N.31.c.6.5.
    N.31.a.8.4.
    N.31.c.00.55.
    N.31.a.30.68.
    At 2 Strong Points N. of FLERS.
    N.25.b.25.75.

All Strong Points will be garrisoned by a platoon of not less than 25 rifles, and a Lewis or Vickers Gun.

VICKERS GUNS. **16.** O.C. 123rd M.G. Coy. will detail 2 Vickers Guns to
LEWIS GUNS. each Battalion. The remaining 8 guns will remain in
STOKES GUNS. their position of assembly with 11th Queen's as a
Reserve, and will only move on orders received from Brigade Headquarters.

O.C. Battalions will detail 4 men to each Gun to carry ammunition for the Vickers Guns attached to them, and O.C. Queen's will in addition detail 10 men to carry for the reserve guns. These 10 men will report to O.C. 123rd M.G. Coy. at 2 p.m. 14th inst.

O.C. Battalions will detail 2 men to each Lewis Gun to carry drums of ammunition. These should either be carried in buckets or sandbags.

BOMBS. **17.** Every man will carry two MILLS Bombs in his pockets. These are to be looked on as a Reserve for the use of the Bombing Squad, and are to be dumped and collected in each line gained. Each Coy. will detail two Bombing Squads. Each bombing Squad will carry 2 buckets or sandbags full of bombs.

ROCKETS. **18.** Each Battalion will take forward 6 Blue Rockets (S.O.S.)

COMMUNICATION **19.** Every Officer and N.C.O. and 50 men per Coy. will
WITH carry two red flares. These are to be lighted in the
AEROPLANES. front line only, at intervals of 20 yards on gaining the line of each objective, as soon as the contact aeroplane appears, (or calls for flares on the KLAXON Horn) and again at 2 p.m. and 5 p.m. on Z day (15th Sept). and at 7 a.m. on the day following Z day 16th September.
Panels and lamps will also be frequently used to report the situation.

VISUAL SIG- Full use is to be made of Visual Signallers and runners,
NALLING & which may become the only available means of communication.
RUNNING. (a) Visual Signalling.
Messages may be handed in for despatch at the undermentioned Visual Stations:-
    S.18.c.1.9.
    S.16.b.5.2.
    S.16.d.6.1.
    S.27.b.3.0.
    POMMIERS REDOUBT.

(b) Runners.
Each Battalion will add 12 more runners to its present establishment. These runners must be properly organised by the Battalion Signal Officer into relays, each relay working between posts which should give protection from fire. The routes between posts should be definitely marked either by paper or some other means. Each Post should have a distinctive mark.

Each Battalion will send 4 extra runners to report at Brigade H.Q. at 2.30 p.m. 14th inst. to the Brigade Signalling Officer. They will remain at Bde. H.Q. as extra runners.

Runner relay posts have been constructed at intervals of 300 yards in FLARE and MILK LANES.

If other means fail runners must be employed at whatever cost.

5.

PIGEONS. 21. Pigeons, if issued to Battalions, are only to be used if all other means fail, and are for urgent messages only, and must be regarded as a Reserve.

MEDICAL. 22. ADVANCED Dressing Station - THE QUARRY S.22.c.2.6.

Divl. Collecting Station - F.6.a.2.0. MAMETZ - MONTAUBAN ROAD.

LIAISON. 23. The 4 Brigade Liaison Officers will report to the Brigade Major at 2.30 p.m. 14th inst. for orders.

DRESS. 24. Fighting order, 2 sandbags, 2 MILL'S Bombs. Every third man to carry a pick or shovel.
Each man to carry 170 rounds S.A.A.

WATER. 25. Water bottles are to be filled before taking up position of assembly.
Each Battalion will detail a carrying party of 25 men to follow the rear Coy. and each man to carry 2 full petrol tins of water.
It must be impressed on the men that water will be very scarce.

S.A.A. 26. In addition to the 170 rounds carried as per para 24, each Coy. will detail 40 men to carry an extra bandolier.

DUMPS. 27. The positions and contents of dumps are shown in Appendix "D". The 123rd Infantry Brigade as it advances can draw on either dump.
Each Battalion will detail 6 men to report to Lieut DIXON, 20th Durham L.I. at Brigade H.Q. at 6 p.m. 14th inst. They will then be taken to GREEN LANE DUMP, where they will be used as a carrying party when the Brigade advances.

PRISONERS OF WAR. 28. Will be brought back to the nearest Stragglers Post, or will be handed over to the first mounted escort met.
An Escort of 10% is sufficient.
Corps Cage at F.8.c. (MAP 62D).

TRANSPORT. 29. 1st Line Transport will be located at F.2.c. and d.

WATCHES. 30. Synchronised time will be sent by runner at 11 a.m. and 5 p.m. on the 14th inst., and by telephone and runner at 5 a.m. 15th inst.

REPORTS. 31. Reports will be sent to Brigade H.Q. POMMIERS REDOUBT at 0.45 mins. and every hour afterwards.

32. Acknowledge.

September 14th 1916.

HCB Kirkpatrick
Captain,
Brigade Major,
123rd Infantry Brigade.

Issued to Signals at 9.45 as under:-
Copy No.1 Filed.   Copy No.7. 123rd M.G. Coy.
  " No.2 War Diary.   " No.8. 123rd Bde.T.M.B.
  " No.3 G.O.C.   " No.9. 11th Queen's.
  " No.4 Brigade Major,   No.10. 10th R.W. Kent Regt.
  " No.5 Staff Capt.   " No.11 23rd Middlesex Regt.
  " No.6 41st Divn.   " No.12 20th Durham L.I.
                           " No.13   N.Z. Bde.
                           " No.14   Inf. Bde. 14th Div.
                           " No.15. 122nd Inf. Bde.
                           " No.16 124th Inf. Bde.
                           " No.17 123rd Bde. Sig. Officer.
                           " No.18 123rd Bde. Transport Officer.
                           " No.19 233rd Field Coy. R.E.

APPENDIX "A" - ASSEMBLY.

DATE.	UNIT.	TRENCHES TO BE OCCUPIED.	HOUR OF ARRIVAL AT TRENCHES.	HOUR BY WHICH RELIEF IS TO BE COMPLETED.	AVENUE OF APPROACH.	REMARKS.
15th Sept.	23rd Middlesex Regt.	CARLTON TRENCH from S.13.b.5.4. to S.16.b.10.0. Lewis Assembly Trench S.16.b.4.6. to S.16.b.10.4.	1 a.m.	2 a.m.	MILK ~~LANE~~ Alley.	Coys. to march with 300[x] interval.
15th Sept.	10th R.W. Kent Regt.	YORK TRENCH from S.16.d.0.5. to S.15.d.8.1.	1.30 a.m.	2.30 a.m.	FLARE LANE.	do. Room is to be left on either side of Brigade H.Q. in YORK TRENCH.
15th Sept.	20th Durham L.I.	Check Line from S.22.a.6.6. to S.22.b.10.0.	2 a.m.	3 a.m.	FLARE LANE.	The R.F.A. occupy 150 yards of this trench, thus leaving 580 yds. for the Battalion.
15th Sept.	11th Queen's.	MONTAUBAN ALLEY in present position.				

All Battalions will Stand-to, ½ an hour before ZERO hour.

Completion of Relief to be at once reported to Bde H.Q.

11th (S) Bn. "The Queen's" Regiment.

INTELLIGENCE REPORT.

APP. III

Quince occupying MONTAUBAN ALLEY on the 14th inst.
On orders to move they proceeded via MILK LANE to CHARLTON TRENCH at 12 noon, this was occupied until 11 p.m. when Battalion was ordered forward to take over the defences of FLERS.
On arrival at FLERS at 3 a.m. I found mixed parties of the 122 & 124 Brigade holding a line parallel with FLERS. Captain Robinson of the 32nd Royal Fusiliers although injured volunteered to show me strong points in front of FLERS which the enemy had vacated. Thanks to this officer the 11th Queen's were able to consolidate NORTH of FLERS and join up with the 14th Division on the RIGHT and the ANZACS on the LEFT. The work performed by Captain Robinson was of great value and also of great risk as at the time no one knew whether the enemy were occupying FLERS or not. The battalion proceeded to dig in immediately occupying a line at N.25.c.3.2. west through BOX & COX-HOGS HEAD, to road at N.31.d.8.1. Line was dug in by daylight.
During the early morning heavy enemy shelling by guns of all calibres.
At 9.30 a.m. 64th Brigade attempted an attack, which failed with heavy casualties after which line was heavily barraged. Consolidation was carried on when possible.
On the 16th inst. Quad reported to Quince to assist in the defence of FLERS.
In the afternoon further units of the 64th Brigade appeared for a further attack.
During our preparatory barrage enemy were reported advancing and battalion stood to. The attack did not develop.
The units ready for the attack on the German lines did not leave our trenches and thereby caused great overcrowding and delayed work in progress.
Later in the evening reports came in that enemy would counter-

attack at 2 a.m. the 17th.

Thorough preparations were made and battalion stood to at 1.30 a.m.

After waiting till 2.45, normal conditions were resumed, and nothing further occurred in the night.

During the morning and afternoon of the 17th heavy shelling was experienced.

The remainder of the 64th Brigade were still in our front line.

At 2.30 p.m. our artillery commenced a heavy bombardment which was quickly replied to, it became intense at 4 p.m. and continued to 6.30 p.m. Shells of large calibre were falling into the village of FLERS, causing however, no damage of military importance. Tear shells were also used.

At 9.30 p.m. the first units of the relieving Brigade commenced to arrive and relief was complete by about 12.30 a.m. the 18th. Except for occasional shelling of FLERS Village and the Lingeval-Flers road, the night was quiet.

19-9-16

Major.

O.C. IIth (S) Bn. "The Queen's" (R.W.S.) Regiment.

APP. IV   Copy No 1

Orders In the Event of Enemy Counter-Attack.

The Front Line will keep well under parapet during barrage — Sentries only looking out. As soon as barrage lifts the parapet will be manned.

The Front Line and Strong-points must stand firm — the enemy moral is low and will not face the bayonet.

Should the enemy penetrate our front line, the troops on the flanks will immediately bomb him. If O.C Front Line needs the Companys in Support and Reserve to deliver a counter-attack, he will fire 3 Very lights in rapid succession towards the ~~front~~ Support line. The Support Company will at once attack over the top, going through any barrage which might be encountered. The Reserve Company will follow it, and if required, render assistance.

If the enemy penetrates the line on our right or left flanks, the Stokes Gunner must be prepared to shell the line held by the enemy, and the front line would immediately bomb its way along the captured trench. The Support company will stand by to refuse whichever flank is threatened, and the reserve company will be prepared to counter-attack under orders from the O.C. Royal West Kent Regt. or Anyact.

Should the Support or Reserve companies have to counter attack, they must move at once and with determination. On no account must the enemy be given time to consolidate

If the Machine Guns and Lewis Guns can be kept intact and ready to fire, no German counter attack can succeed.

O.C. Coys are reminded that the S.O.S. signal is 3 Blue Rockets

Companies in rear may get no information as to the result of the enemy counter-attack. They must take steps to find out what has happened without fail.

R. Otter Lt. Col.
Commandging Officer.

Copy No 1 to File.
  "   " 2   Bde H.Q.
  "   " 3   O.C. A Coy
  "   " 4   "   B
  "   " 5   "   C
  "   " 6   "   D
  "   " 7   Trench Mortars
  "   " 8   Machine Gun Coy
  "   " 9   O.C. R.W.K.
  "   " 10   O.C. Ompecs.

TIME TABLE OF ATTACK.

Before Zero. Tanks start as required in order to reach SWITCH Line at 0.25 minutes east of LONGUEVAL - FLERS ROAD, and at 0.15 minutes west of that road.

0.00 (Zero) Infantry leave their trenches and advance close up to the barrage which will begin creeping back in front of them at 0.6 minutes.
Creeping barrage will go back steadily at 50 yards per minute until it joins stationary barrage on first objective (green line).

0.15 minutes. Tanks reach positions of first objective west of FLERS ROAD.

0.25 minutes. Tanks reach positions of first objective east of FLERS ROAD.

(i) 0.20 minutes (i) Barrage lifts from green line west of FLERS ROAD.
(ii) 0.30 minutes (ii) Barrage lifts from green line east of FLERS Road. - Infantry capture first objective as the barrage lifts in each case. Creeping barrage halts 300 yards beyond green line.

1 hour 00 minutes. Infantry and tanks advance together behind creeping barrage. Creeping barrage goes back 100 yards in three minutes, and on arrival at FLERS LINE joins stationary barrage.

1 hour 25 minutes. Barrage lifts from second objective of 14th. and 41st Divisions. 14th. and 41st.Divisions capture brown line.

1 hour 30 minutes. Barrage lifts from second objective of New Zealand Division. New Zealand Division captures brown line.

1 hour 45 minutes. Covering barrage goes back to allow tanks to advance from brown line.

2 hours 00 minutes. Infantry advance, complete capture of FLERS, and establish the blue line.

4 hours 15 minutes. Covering barrage taken off to allow tanks to go forward.

(i) 4 hrs.30 min.   ) barrage lifts from ((i) Right boundary and Road N 32 b 30.
(ii) 4 hrs.55 mins.) GIRD TRENCH & GIRD ((ii) Road N 32 b 38 and track N 26 c 45.
(iii) 5 hrs.00 mins.) SUPPORT between ((iii) Track N 26 c 45 and left boundary.

5 hrs. 30 mins. Bombardment of GUEUDECOURT ceases - Tanks push forward, and infantry complete capture of fourth objective.

APPENDIX B.

MILLS BOMBS. .... to complete to 2 per man.

"P" Grenades. .... 80 per Battalion.

Rockets. .... 6 per Battalion.

Red Flares. .... 390 per Battalion.

Stokes Gun Ammunition.... 100 Rounds to be taken to assembly trenches in handcarts. *per Regt.*

Bomb Buckets. .... 40.

Shovels and Picks. ...... to complete to 1 every 3rd. man.

Sandbags. .... 2 per man.

S.A.A. .... 8 boxes per Battalion.

TABLE 3.
SITUATION AND CONTENTS OF DUMPS.
SITUATION.

Main Divisional Dump .... F 7 a 0 3.

Right Bde. Dump .... S23 a 6 8.

Left Bde. Dump. (known as GREEN DUMP) .... S16 d 0 6.

CONTENTS.

Nature of Store.	Each Bde Dump.
No.5 MILLS Grenades.	5,000.
STOKES 3" bombs.	2,000.
Red cartridges.	2,000.
Green Cartridges.	2,000.
1" VERY Lights.	1,000.
1½" Very Lights.	500.
2" Trench Mortar.	250.
S.A.A. (boxes).	100.
"P" Grenades.	500.
Rifle Grenades.	1,000.
Rockets "S.O.S." and sticks.	25. ::
Fl res red.	--
Petrol Tins, 2 gallons.	400.

::   This includes those issued under Brigade Orders to units in the line.

New Work
13-9-16

Main Communication
trenches in blue

(DIV. 2)
Scale 1:10,000
Tuesday,
12-9-16.
The thick line
represents the
British Front.
o o o are
Strong points

C Coy D Coy
DISPOSITIONS
28th and 29th Sept. 1916.

B Coy

A Coy

Gueudecourt

25

B Coy 100 D Coy
     20

C Coy A Coy
H.Q.

Maps 57c S.W.1.
57c S.W.3.
Scale 1:10,000

JOIN

WAR DIARY or INTELLIGENCE SUMMARY

11TH BN THE QUEEN'S REGT.
1ST – 31ST OCTOBER 1916

Army Form C. 2118

123/41

Original

Place	Date	Hour	Summary of Events and Information	Remarks and references to Appendices
FLERS	1/10/16	9 p.m.	The battalion was relieved by the 7th Bn. King's Own Regiment, and moved into bivouac near POMMIER REDOUBT.	
POMMIERS	2/10/16	1 p.m.	The battalion moved into bivouac near MAMETZ WOOD where it remained until 7th inst.	
MAMETZ WOOD	7/10/16	7 a.m.	In accordance with 123rd Infy Brigade Order No. 36, the battalion moved off to occupy FLERS TRENCH. But, owing to the heavy shelling of that trench, which was in progress when the battalion arrived, permission was obtained to occupy ~~jus~~ SRD SWITCH TRENCH. The battalion then moved into occupation of FLERS TRENCH, FLERS TURK LANE to GOOSE ALLEY with 1 company (A Coy) EAST of TURK LANE.	APP I
		9 p.m.	D Coy was sent to occupy part of GIRD SUPPORT on right of the ~~Queens~~ 26th Royal Fusiliers.	
FLERS TRENCH	8/10/16		Misc Infantry. Quiet day. Four shells fell near the trench, though the enemy howies were firing at our batteries in rear all day.	
	9/10/16	4 a.m.	D Coy was relieved and returned to FLERS TRENCH. Working parties & fatigues were found by the battalion for the front line.	

Army Form C. 2118

WAR DIARY
or
INTELLIGENCE SUMMARY
(Erase heading not required.)

Instructions regarding War Diaries and Intelligence Summaries are contained in F.S. Regs., Part II. and the Staff Manual respectively. Title Pages will be prepared in manuscript.

Place	Date	Hour	Summary of Events and Information	Remarks and references to Appendices
FLERS	10/10/16	9 p.m.	The battalion was relieved by the 19th King's Regiment, and relieved Ithionas near Mametz Wood. The it remained until 13th.	
MAMETZ WOOD	13/10/16	7 a.m.	Battalion entrained for Dernan Court, where it was billetted in the village.	
DERNAN COURT	17/10/16	12 noon	Entrained for Oisemont, and marched to Limeux the following day.	
LIMEUX	19/10/16	2 p.m.	Left by march route for Pont Remy, where the battalion entrained for Godewaersvelde.	
GODEWAERSVELDE	20/10/16	6 a.m.	Left by march route to Chippewa Camp.	
CHIPPEWA CAMP	23/10/16	3.30 p.m.	Relieved 62nd Battalion Australian I.F. Trenches O.33 & O.41. 7th London Regiment, 47th Division on the left and 23rd Middlesex on the right. Companies were located as under:- 'A' Coy T. O33 - O36 'B' Coy Lock House 'C' T. O37 - O41 'D' Coy Old French Trench. Bn HdQrs. Spoil Bank.	APP II
			Nothing of importance occurred during this tour of duty.) The enemy	

Place	Date	Hour	Summary of Events and Information	Remarks and references to Appendices
Trenches	28/10/16	7 pm	Shelled the trenches with a few minenwerfen daily, damaging the trenches, which were almost unfamed. The wind was in a dangerous quarter all the time. Retaliation was obtained from R.F.A. and L.T.M.B. Battalion was relieved by 11th Bn Royal West Kent Regiment, & moved into huts near RENINGHELST. (Map Ref M 5.a.3.3) Casualties during the tour in trenches 1 man killed & 1 wounded. Casualties during the month. Killed O.R. 16. Wounded O.R. 43. Missing O.R. 4. —— 63 —— R. Oxx Lt.Col. Cmdg 11th Bn PnQueens	

APP I

All Coys, Quinns.   8.10.16

In the event of coys having to ~~support~~ the front line, coys will move as follows. A & B Coys via TURK LANE, C & D via GOOSE ALLEY. O.C. Coys will send guides to find out the way to Battalion Head Quarters of Quad & Quill, in front line. Coys will move to wherever they are needed independently on receiving instructions from this office. O.C. Coys will report in person to whichever Bn H.Qrs they are ordered to support. Bn H.Q. will not move, unless ordered, in which case coys will be informed.

R.C.Smith Capt & Adj.

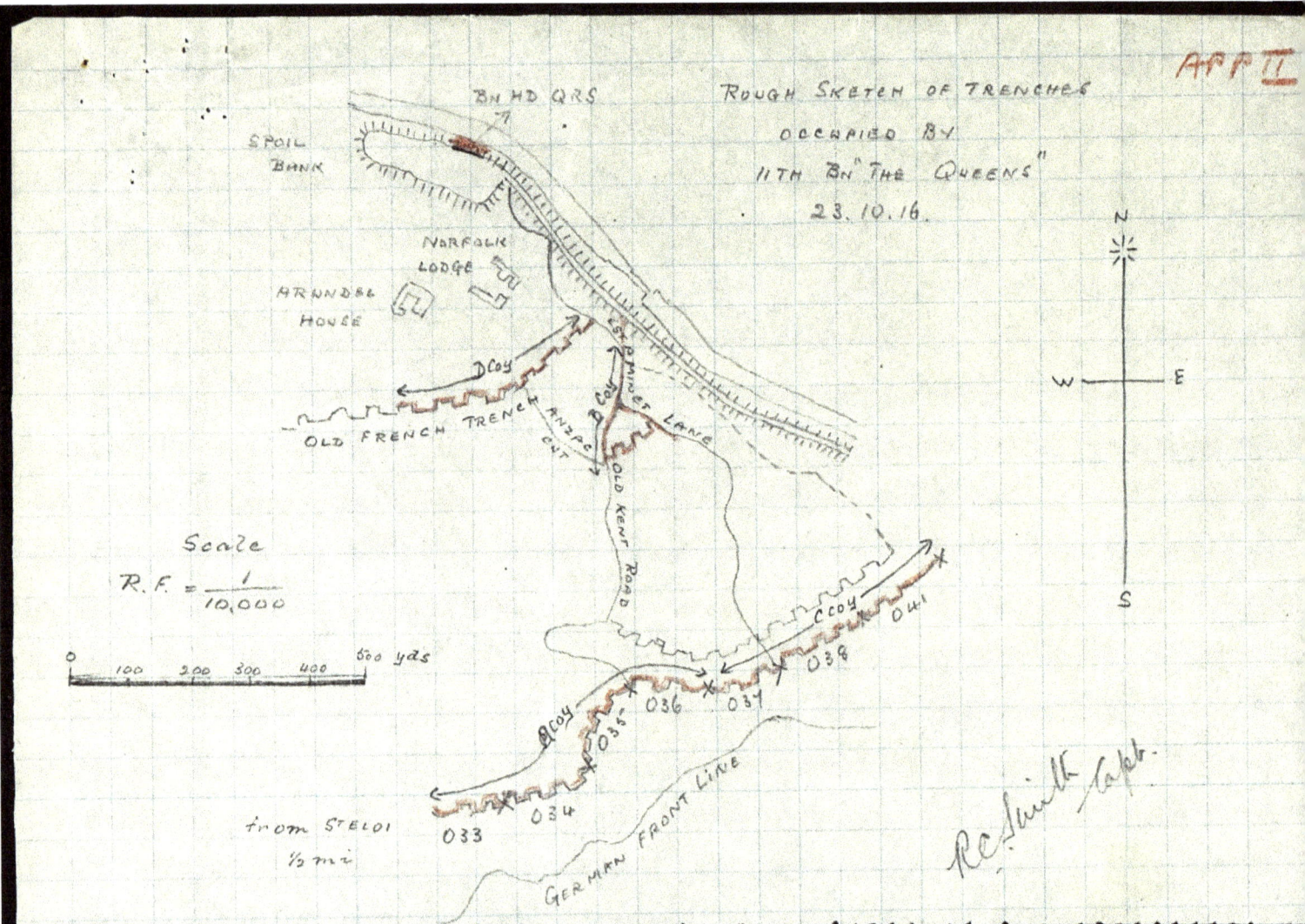

11TH (S) BN THE QUEENS (R.W.S.) Regt

WEEKLY STRENGTH RETURN

	Killed		Wounded		Missing		Evacuated Sick		Sent to Base		Struck off other purposes		Officers notified Struck off		TOTAL Struck off		Reinforcements	
	Off	O.R.	Off	O.R.	Off	O.R.	Off	O.R.	Off	O.R.	Off	O.R.	Off	O.R.	Off	O.R.	Off	O.R.
SUNDAY 1st	-	17	1	69	-	1	-	-	-	-	-	-	-	-	1	87	-	-
MONDAY 2nd	-	-	-	-	-	1	-	-	-	-	-	-	-	1	-	2	-	-
TUESDAY 3rd	-	-	-	-	-	-	-	-	-	-	-	-	-	-	-	-	-	3
WEDNESDAY 4th	-	-	-	-	-	-	-	-	-	-	-	-	-	-	-	-	-	-
THURSDAY 5th	-	-	-	-	-	-	-	-	-	-	-	-	-	-	-	-	-	-
FRIDAY 6th	-	-	-	1	-	-	-	-	-	-	-	-	-	-	-	-	-	1
SATURDAY 7th	-	-	-	-	-	2	-	-	-	-	-	-	-	-	-	-	-	-
	-	17	1	70	-	2									1	89	-	4

+ Excludes those "slightly at duty"

DETAILS OVER.

	OFFICERS	O.R.
Strength last week	26	892
Deduct struck off		89
Remaining		803
Add reinforcements		4
Strength this week	25	807

7th October 1916

R.C. Shields Capt for Lt Col
Commdg. 11th Bn "The Queens" R.W.S. Regt.

Nature of Work	Officers	O.R.
Divisional Rest & F.A.		37
Road Control		3
Divisional Salvage	1	1
A.S.C. Loaders		2
Intelligence Dept		1
Divisional Headquarters		5
Brigade Salvage		2
123rd Brigade		8
Battn. Storeman at Steenwerck		1
	1	60

11TH (S) BN THE QUEEN'S (R.W.S.) Regt.

WEEKLY STRENGTH RETURN

	Killed		Wounded+		Missing		Evacuated Sick		Sent to Base		Struck off other purposes		Officers notified Struck off		TOTAL Struck off		Reinforcements	
	Off	O.R.	Off	O.R.	Off	O.R.	Off	O.R.	Off	O.R.	Off	O.R.	Off	O.R.	Off	O.R.	Off	O.R.
SUNDAY 8th	—	8	—	15	—	1	—	—	—	—	—	—	—	—	—	24	—	4
MONDAY 9th	—	1	—	1	—	1	—	—	—	—	—	—	—	—	—	2	—	17
TUESDAY 10th	—	1	—	1	—	—	—	—	—	—	—	—	—	—	—	2	—	—
WEDNESDAY 11th	—	—	—	—	—	—	—	—	—	—	—	—	—	1	—	1	4	—
THURSDAY 12th	—	—	—	—	—	—	—	—	—	—	—	—	—	—	—	—	—	—
FRIDAY 13th	—	—	—	—	—	—	—	—	—	—	—	—	—	—	—	1	—	18
SATURDAY 14th	—	—	—	—	—	—	—	2	—	—	—	—	—	—	—	1	—	—
	—	10	—	16	—	2	—	—	—	—	—	—	—	1	—	28	4	39

+ Excludes those "slightly at duty"

DETAILS OVER.

	OFFICERS.	O.R.
Strength last week	25	802
Deduct struck off	—	28
Remaining	25	774
Add Reinforcements	4	39
Strength this week	29	813

14th October 1916

Re Lieut. Capt. for Lt Col.

Commdg. 11th Bn. The Queen's R.W.S. Regt.

Nature of Work	Officers	O.R.
Divisional Rest & F.A.		33
Road Control		3
Divisional Salvage	1	1
A.S.C. Loaders		2
Intelligence Dept		1
Divisional Headquarters		5
Brigade Salvage		2
123rd Brigade		8
Battalion Storeman (at Sternwerck)		1
	1	56

11TH (S) BN THE QUEENS (R.W.S.) REGT

WEEKLY STRENGTH RETURN

	Killed		Wounded/Missing +		Evacuated Sick		Sent to Base		Struck off other purposes		Officers sick/listed Struck off		TOTAL Struck off		Reinforcements	
	Off	O.R.	Off	O.R.	Off	O.R.	Off	O.R.	Off	O.R.	Off	O.R.	Off	O.R.	Off	O.R.
SUNDAY 15																
MONDAY 16																3
TUESDAY 17																
WEDNESDAY 18												1		1		
THURSDAY 19																
FRIDAY 20																
SATURDAY 21												1		1		3

+ Excludes those "slightly at duty"

DETAILS OVER.

	OFFICERS.	O.R.
Strength last week	29	818
Deduct struck off	1	—
Remaining	28	818
Add Reinforcements		3
Strength this week.	28	821

21st October 1916

R. Schulk Capt for Lt Col
Commndg. 11th Bn The Queens R.W.S. Regt.

Nature of Work	Officers	O.R.
Divisional Rest & F.A.		38
Road Control		3
Divisional Salvage	1	1
A.S.C. Loaders		2
Intelligence Dept		1
Divisional Headquarters		5
Brigade Salvage		2
123rd Brigade		8
Battn. Storeman (at Steenwerck)		1
	1	61

11TH (S) BN THE QUEENS (R.W.S) REGT

WEEKLY STRENGTH RETURN

	Killed		Wounded		Missing		Evacuated Sick		Sent to Base		Struck off other purposes		Officers notified Struck off		Total Struck †		Reinforcements	
	Off	O.R.	Off	O.R.	Off	O.R.	Off	O.R.	Off	O.R.	Off	O.R.	Off	O.R.	Off	O.R.	Off	O.R.
SUNDAY 22nd																		
MONDAY 23rd																		
TUESDAY 24th																		
WEDNESDAY 25th																		
THURSDAY 26th		1						1								3		
FRIDAY 27th																		
SATURDAY 28th		1		1				1								3		

† Excludes those "slightly at duty"

DETAILS OVER.

	OFFICERS.	O.R.
Strength last week	28	821
Deduct struck off	—	3
Remaining	28	818
Add Reinforcements this week	—	—
Strength this week.	28	818

1 T.M.B.
1 M.O.
1 CHAP.
——
31

3 ORC.
12 T.M.B.
——
833

28th October 1916

R C Shuttleworth Lt Col
Commdg. 11th Bn. The Queens R.W.S. Regt

Nature of Work	Officers	OR.
Divisional Rest & F.A.	1	41
Road Control		5
Divisional Salvage	1	1
A. S. C. Loaders		2
Intelligence Dept.		1
Divisional Headquarters		5
Brigade Salvage		2
123rd Brigade		8
Battn. Storeman (at Stirsanvick)		1
	2	66

WAR DIARY or INTELLIGENCE SUMMARY

11TH BN "THE QUEENS"
1st to 30th Nov. 1916.

Place	Date	Hour	Summary of Events and Information	Remarks and references to Appendices
RENINGHELST	2nd Nov.		The battalion relieved the 11th Royal West Kent Regiment in the front line, the same dispositions as before.	
TRENCHES	4th Nov.		Our Artillery and Trench Mortars bombarded the enemy's lines, and cut their wire in several places. Retaliation effects some material damage to OLD KENT ROAD.	
	8th Nov.		Very little of importance occurred during this tour in the trenches. The 2 Support Companies were chiefly employed in carrying parties of various natures, and the front line companies in repairing the parapet, drainage etc. During the afternoon, the battalion was relieved by the 11th Bn R.W. Kents, and returned to the same huts previously occupied at RENINGHELST.	
RENINGHELST	9th - 14th Nov.		The men were employed on working-parties under the R.E. Battery, and cleaning up generally. Battalion schools were also formed in wiring, Lewis Guns, bombing, firing and signalling.	
RENINGHELST	15th Nov	5.35 p.m.	The battalion relieved the 11th R.W. Kent in the line, the relief being completed by 5.35 p.m. On the way through DICKEBUCH, 2 shells fell among the men of 'C' Coy who were having dinners. 5 men were killed - Serient. Lieut Corporals F.M. TODD and A. TUGWELL and eleven men were wounded.	

Army Form C. 2118

WAR DIARY
or
INTELLIGENCE SUMMARY
(Erase heading not required.)

Instructions regarding War Diaries and Intelligence Summaries are contained in F. S. Regs., Part II. and the Staff Manual respectively. Title Pages will be prepared in manuscript.

Place	Date	Hour	Summary of Events and Information	Remarks and references to Appendices
	Nov 22nd		Nothing of importance reveal during this tour of duty. Work was continued in making strong points in D33 & O41, also a machine gun emplacement. Medium Trench Mortars bombarded the enemy's wire torn effect, but the enemy's retaliation also caused us some damage, which took time & labour to repair. The weather was very cold, and the last day or two we were at Hallvin. The battalion was relieved by the 11th R.W. Kent, and returned to the same hutments.	
RENINGHELST	23rd			
	24th		The whole battalion was on working parties from 10 a.m. The weather very bad. There had been wet baths, and general clean up.	
	27th		Relieve 11th R.W. Kent Regiment in the trenches. Nothing to report has occurred. The work on strong points is being proceeded with.	
			Casualties during the week were Killed — O.R. 5 Died of Wounds — O.R. 1 Wounded — Officers 2 O.R. 16	

1. XII. 16

R Otte
Lt Col.
Cmdg 11th Bn The Queens Regt

1875 Wt. W593/826 1,000,000 4/15 J.B.C. & A. A.D.S.S./Forms/C. 2118.

11TH (S) BN. THE QUEENS (RWS) REGT

WEEKLY STRENGTH RETURN.

	KILLED.		+ WOUNDED		MISSING		EVACUATED SICK		SENT TO BASE		STRUCK OFF OTHER PURPOSES		OFFICERS NOTIFIED STRUCK OFF		TOTAL STRUCK OFF		REINFORCEMENTS	
	Off.	O.R.	Off.	O.R.	Off.	O.R.	Off.	O.R.	Off.	O.R.	Off.	O.R.	Off.	O.R.	Off.	O.R.	Off.	O.R.
SUNDAY 29				1 28/10/16				1 28/10/16										
MONDAY 30																	1	3
TUESDAY 31												4						
WEDNESDAY 1																		
THURSDAY 2																		
FRIDAY 3																		
SATURDAY 4				1				1				4					1	3

+ Excludes those "slightly at duty"

DETAILS.	OFFICERS.	O.R.
Strength last week.	28	818
Deduct Struck off.	1	5
Remaining	27	813
Add Reinforcement	1	3
Strength this week.	28	818
	1 I.M.S.	3 O.R.C. &c
	1 M.O.	12 J.M.S
	1 CHAP	831
	31	

November 1916.

R.C.Smith Lt.Col.
Commdg 11th Bn. "The Queens" R.W.S. Regt.

NATURE OF WORK.	Officers.	O. R.
Divisional Rest & F.A.	2	51.
Road Control.		5.
Divisional Salvage.	1	1.
A.S.C.Leaders.		2.
Intelligence Dept.		1.
On Courses	1	7
Brigade Salvage		2.
123rd Brigade H.Q. & Divisional H.Q.		37.
123rd T.M.Battery	1.	20.
123rd M.G.Company	1.	14.
1st Canadian Tunnelling Coy.		6.
250th Coy. R.E.		2.
R.E.Corps Park		7.
	6	161.

11TH (S) BN. "THE QUEEN'S" (R.W.S.) REGT.

WEEKLY STRENGTH RETURN

	Killed		Wounded †		Missing		Evacuated Sick		Sent to Base		Struck off other purposes		Officers notified Struck off		Total Struck off		Reinforcements	
	Off.	O.R.	Off.	O.R.	Off.	O.R.	Off.	O.R.	Off.	O.R.	Off.	O.R.	Off.	O.R.	Off.	O.R.	Off.	O.R.
Sunday 5th	—	—	—	—	—	—	—	1	—	—	—	—	—	1	—	1	—	—
Monday 6th	—	—	—	1	—	—	—	2	—	1	—	—	—	—	—	2	—	—
Tuesday 7th	—	—	—	—	—	—	—	1	—	—	—	—	—	—	—	1	—	1
Wednesday 8th	—	—	—	—	—	—	—	—	—	—	—	—	—	—	—	—	—	—
Thursday 9th	—	—	—	—	—	—	—	—	—	—	—	—	—	—	—	—	—	4
Friday 10th	—	—	—	—	—	—	—	—	—	—	—	—	—	—	—	—	—	—
Saturday 11th	—	—	—	1	—	—	—	2	—	2	—	—	—	2	—	3	1	5

† Excludes those "slightly at duty"

Strength last week
Deduct Struck off
Remaining
Add reinforcements
Strength this week

	Officers	O.R.
	28	816
	2	3
	26	813
	1	5
	27	818

Details over

11th November 1916

P. Otter Lt Col.
Commdg. 11th Bn "The Queen's" R.W.S. Regt.

Nature of Work.	Officers	O.R.
Divisional Rest & F.A.	1	59
Road Control		3
Divisional Salvage	1	1
A.S.C. Loaders		2
Intelligence Dept.		1
On Courses	2	11
Brigade Salvage		2
Bde & Divl. Hd. Qrs.		30
123rd T.M. Battery		19
123rd M.G. Coy	1	12
1st Cand. Tunnelling Coy.		6
250th Coy R.E.		8
R.E. Corp Park		7
10th Corps H.Q.		9
	5	170

11(S) Bn The Queens (R.W.S.) Regt

WEEKLY STRENGTH RETURN

	Killed		Wounded/Missing			Evacuated Sick		Sent to Base		Struck off other Reasons		Officers Struck off taken		Total Struck Off		Not Present		
	Off	O.R.	Off	O.R.		Off	O.R.	Off	O.R.	Off	O.R.	Off	O.R.	Off	O.R.	Off	O.R.	
Sunday 12th	—	—	—	—		—	—	—	16	—	—	—	—	—	16	—	2	
Monday 13th	—	—	—	1		—	—	—	1	—	—	—	—	—	1	—	—	
Tuesday 14th	—	—	—	1		—	—	—	1	—	—	—	—	—	1	—	—	
Wednesday 15th	—	4	2	10		—	—	—	—	—	—	—	—	2	14	—	—	
Thursday 16th	—	—	—	3		—	—	—	—	—	—	—	—	—	3	—	—	
Friday 17th	—	—	—	5		—	—	—	—	—	—	—	—	—	5	—	—	
Saturday 18th	—	—	—	—		—	—	—	1	—	—	—	—	—	1	—	—	
	—	4	2	18		—	—	—	18	—	—	—	—	2	40	—	2	

	Off	O.R.
Strength last week	27	818
Struck off	2	40
	25	778
	1	2
	26	780

R.C. Shute Capt for
Formerly 11th Bn The Queens (R.W.S.) Regt

18th

Nature of Works.	Officers	O.R.
Divl. Rest & J.A.	1	54
Road Control		3
Divl. Salvage	1	1
A.S.C. Loaders.		2
Intelligence		1
On Courses	2	26
Bde Salvage		2
" & Divl Headquarters	1	39
123. T.M. Batty		19
" M.G. Coy.		11
1st Canadian Tunnelling Co		6
250th Coy R.E.		8
R.E. Corps Park		7
10th Corps. Hd. Qrs.		9
On Leave	2	6
	7	194

11th Bn THE QUEEN'S (R.W.S.) Regiment

WEEKLY STRENGTH RETURN

	Killed		Wounded #		Missing		Evacuated Sick		Sent to Base		Struck off Other Purposes		Officer Notified Struck off		Total Struck off		Reinforcements	
	OFF	O.R.	OFF	O.R.	OFF	O.R.	OFF	O.R.	OFF	O.R.	OFF	O.R.	OFF	O.R.	OFF	O.R.	OFF	O.R.
Sunday 19th	—	—	—	—	—	—	—	—	—	—	—	—	—	—	—	—	3	6
Monday 20th	—	—	—	—	—	—	—	18	—	—	—	—	—	—	—	18	—	—
Tuesday 21st	—	—	—	—	—	—	—	—	—	—	—	—	—	—	—	—	—	—
Wednesday 22nd	—	—	—	—	—	—	—	—	—	—	—	—	—	—	—	—	—	2
Thursday 23rd	—	—	—	—	—	—	—	—	—	—	—	—	—	—	—	—	—	—
Friday 24th	—	—	—	—	—	—	—	—	—	—	—	—	—	—	—	—	—	—
Saturday 25th	—	—	—	—	—	—	—	—	—	—	—	—	—	—	—	—	—	—
TOTAL	—	—	—	—	—	—	—	18	—	—	—	—	—	—	—	18	3	8

\# Exclude those "slightly at duty"

	OFFICER	O.R.
Strength last week	25	780
Deduct struck off	—	18
Remaining	25	762
Add Reinforcements	3	8
Strength this week	28	770

Details over.

25th November 1916

Ashwith Coffer Major
Commdg. 11th Bn The Queen's (R.W.S.) Regt

Nature of Work	Officers	O.R
Divl Rest & J.A.	1	48
Road Control		3
Divl Salvage	1	1
A.S.C. Loaders		2
Intelligence		1
On Course	5	29
Bde Salvage		2
" & Divl Headquarters	1	25
123rd T.M.B		17
" M.G. Coy		7
1st Can Tunnelling Co		6
250th Coy R.E.		8
R.E. Corp Park		7
10th Corp Hd Qrs		9
On Leave	2	8
Fatigue Party at Brigade School.	1	29
	11	202

WAR DIARY
or
INTELLIGENCE SUMMARY

(Erase heading not required.)

Army Form C. 2118

11th Bn The Queen's Regiment

1.12.16 – 31.12.16.

Vol 8

Place	Date	Hour	Summary of Events and Information	Remarks and references to Appendices
TRENCHES	2/12/16	—	Battalion was relieved by 11th Royal West Kent Regiment and returned to billets in ALBERTA CAMP, RENINGHELST.	
RENINGHELST	8/12/16	—	Relieved 11th Bn Royal West Kent Regiment in the Trenches.	
	11/12/16	—	A camouflet was blown by the division on our left. About half-an-hour after a raid of about half-an-hour with minenwerfers relapsed. During the night the enemy gave sharp bursts of fire intermittently. The only casualties however was 1 killed and 1 wounded. Much damage was done to OLD KENT ROAD & SOMMINET LANE. Nothing however of special interest occurred during the tour of the trenches. The increase of the enemy's artillery activity was most marked until the battalion was relieved by 11th Royal West Kent on 14th December.	
RENINGHELST	16/12/16	—	A draft of 2 officers (Sec. Lieuts. A.E. JOYNER and W.H.F. COURTHOPE) and 184 men (of chiefly yeomen).	
	19/12/16	—	Sec Lt T. MARTIN joined the battalion.	

Army Form C. 2118

WAR DIARY
or
INTELLIGENCE SUMMARY
(Erase heading not required.)

Instructions regarding War Diaries and Intelligence Summaries are contained in F.S. Regs., Part II. and the Staff Manual respectively. Title Pages will be prepared in manuscript.

Place	Date	Hour	Summary of Events and Information	Remarks and references to Appendices
RENINGHELST	21/12/16	—	The Battalion was present when the 123rd Infantry Brigade was inspected by the Commander-in-chief, General Sir Douglas Haig. After which it relieved the 1st Royal West Kent in the trenches.	
	23/12/16	—	For operations carried out by 49th Division on the left, the enemy retaliated on our front support lines, and badly damaged the trench at Dick Bogh House as well as ESTAMINET LANE, and OLD KENT ROAD. The front line parapet was also badly blown in. Casualties were 9 wounded (1 of whom was since died of wounds). Enemy Trench Mortars & artillery were active in the early morning.	
	25/12/16	—	Our Artillery and Stokes Guns bombarded their line intermittently throughout the day. Otherwise very quiet.	
	26/12/16	—	Battalion was relieved by the R.W. Kent Regt. & returned to ALBERTA CAMP. Casualties during the month — KILLED 2 WOUNDED 15.	Drafts received 194.

R. Otter Lt.Col.
Cmdg 11 Bn. R.W. Surreys

11th Bn "THE QUEENS" (R.W.S.) REGT.

WEEKLY STRENGTH RETURN

	Killed		Wounded		Missing		Evacuated Sick		Struck off other purposes		Officers notified struck off		Sent to Base		TOTAL struck off		Reinforcements	
	OFF.	O.R.	OFF.	O.R.	OFF.	O.R.	OFF.	O.R.	OFF.	O.R.	OFF.	O.R.	OFF.	O.R.	OFF.	O.R.	OFF.	O.R.
SUNDAY 26		1																6
MONDAY 27			1					4						1	1	5		
TUESDAY 28				1										1		1		
WEDNESDAY 29																		
THURSDAY 30									1				1			1		
FRIDAY 1																		
SATURDAY 2		1		1						4				1	1	7		6

+ Excludes those "slightly at duty"

DETAILS OVER.

	OFFICERS	O.R.
Strength last week		
Deduct struck off		
Remaining		
Add Reinforcements		
Strength this week		

1916.

Robert M. Taylor Lt. Col.
Commanding 11th Bn "The Queens" (R.W.S.) Regt.

Nature of Work	OFFICERS	O.R.
Attcd Brig & Divl HQ.	2	31
" A.S.C.		2
Road Control		3
Divl Salvage	1	1
Intelligence		1
On Course	6	42
Bde Salvage		2
123rd T.M. Battery		17
1st Can Tunnel Co		6
250th Coy R.E's		8
10th Corp H.Q.		9
R.E. Corp Park		7
On Leave to England	2	16
Attached to Bde School	1	4
Divl Rest & F.A.	2	47
TOTAL	13	196

11th Bn The Queen's (R.W.S.) Regt.

WEEKLY STRENGTH RETURN

	Killed		Wounded†		Missing		Evacuated Sick		Struck off other causes		Officers notified struck off		Sent to Base		TOTAL struck off		REINFORCEMENT	
	OFF	O.R	OFF	O.R	OFF	O.R	OFF	O.R	OFF	O.R	OFF	O.R	OFF	O.R	OFF	O.R	OFF	O.R
SUNDAY 3rd																	1	5
MONDAY 4th																		
TUESDAY 5th																		
WEDNESDAY 6th							4								4			
THURSDAY 7th																		
FRIDAY 8th																		
SATURDAY 9th																		3
							4								4	1		8

† Excludes those "slightly at duty"

DETAILS OVER.

	OFFICERS	O.R.
Strength last week	28	769
Deduct struck off		4
Remaining	28	765
Add Reinforcements	1	8
Strength this week	29	773

9th December 1916.

Total 31 / 788

A.R.Whart 2/Lt
Actg Adjt

[signature] Lt Col
Commandg. 11th Bn "The Queen's" (R.W.S.) Regt.

Major

Nature of Work.	OFFICERS	O.R.
Attd. Brigade & Divs		38
" A. & C.		2
Road Control		3
Div. Salvage	1	1
Intelligence		1
On Courses	6	43
Brigade Salvage		2
125th F.N. Battery		17
1st Can Tunnel Coy.		6
250th Coy. R.E.		8
10th Corps A.C.		7
R.E. Corps Park		9
Div. Rest & S.A.	2	44
On Leave	4	21
	15	202.

11th Bn THE QUEEN'S (R.W.S.) REGT

WEEKLY STRENGTH RETURN

	Killed		Wounded		Missing		Evacuated Sick		Struck off other than above		Officers notified struck off		Sent to Base +		TOTAL Struck off		REINFORCEMENT	
	OFF	O.R	OFF	O.R	OFF	O.R	OFF	O.R	OFF	O.R	OFF	O.R	OFF	O.R	OFF	O.R	OFF	O.R
SUNDAY 10th	—	—	—	1	—	—	—	—	—	—	—	—	—	1	—	2	—	—
MONDAY 11th	—	1	—	1	—	—	—	—	—	—	—	—	—	—	—	2	—	6
TUESDAY 12th	—	—	—	—	—	—	—	—	—	—	—	—	—	—	—	—	—	—
WEDNESDAY 13th	—	—	—	2	—	—	—	—	—	—	—	—	—	—	—	2	—	—
THURSDAY 14th	—	—	—	—	—	—	—	—	—	—	—	—	—	—	—	—	1	—
FRIDAY 15th	—	—	—	—	—	—	—	—	—	1	—	—	—	—	1	—	—	—
SATURDAY 16th	—	1	—	4	—	—	—	—	—	1	—	—	—	1	1	6	1	6

+ Excludes those "slightly at duty"

DETAILS OVER.

	OFFICERS	O.R.
Strength last week	29	773
Deduct struck off	—	6
Remaining	29	767
Add Reinforcements	—	6
Strength this week	29	773

16th December 1916

R. Schulte Lt/Col. Major
Commanding 11th Bn "The Queen's" (R.W.S.) Regt.

Nature of Work	Officers	O.R.
Att'd Bde & Div	1	28
" A.S.C.		2
Road Control		8
Div. Salvage	1	1
Intelligence		2
On Course	4	38
Brigade Salvage		2
123rd T.M. Batty.		16
1 Can Tunnell Coy		6
250th Coy R.E.		8
10th Corp. H.Q.		1
R.E. Corp Park		7
Div. Rest. F.A.	2	48
On Leave	4	11
187th Bde R.F.A.		1
	12	174

11th Bn THE QUEEN'S R.W.S.Regt.

WEEKLY STRENGTH RETURN

	Killed		Wounded†		Missing		Evacuated Sick		Struck off other towpowers		Officers notified Struck off		Sent to Base		TOTAL Struck off		REINFORCEMENT	
	OFF	O.R	OFF	O.R	OFF	O.R	OFF	O.R	OFF	O.R	OFF	O.R	OFF	O.R	OFF	O.R	OFF	O.R
SUNDAY 17th	-	-	-	-	-	-	-	1	-	-	-	-	-	-	-	1	2	194
MONDAY 18th	-	-	-	-	-	-	1	-	-	-	-	-	-	-	1	-	-	-
TUESDAY 19th	-	-	-	-	-	-	-	8	-	-	-	-	-	-	-	8	1	-
WEDNESDAY 20th	-	-	-	-	-	-	1	-	-	-	-	-	-	-	1	-	-	-
THURSDAY 21st	-	-	-	-	-	-	-	-	-	-	-	-	-	-	-	-	-	-
FRIDAY 22nd	-	-	-	-	-	-	-	-	-	-	-	-	-	-	-	-	-	-
SATURDAY 23rd	-	-	-	-	-	-	2	9	-	-	-	-	-	-	2	9	3	197

† Excludes those "slightly at duty"

DETAILS OVER.

	OFFICERS	O.R.
Strength last week	28	773
Deduct Struck off	2	9
Remaining	26	764
Add Reinforcements	3	197
Strength this week.	30	961

23rd December 1916.

Neville Capt for Lt.Col.
Commands. 11th Bn "The Queens" (R.W.S.) Regt.

Nature of Work	Officers	O.R.
Att'd Brigade & Division	2	32
" A.S.C.		2
Road Control		3
Div'l Salvage	1	1
Intelligence		1
On Courses	3	36
Brigade Salvage		2
123rd T.M. Battery		16
1st Can Tunnel Coy.		6
250th Coy R.E.		8
10th Corp H.Q.		1
R.E. Corp. Park		7
Div'l Rest & F.A.	2	45
On leave	1	2
187th Bde R.F.A.		1
2nd Army School		1
Draft at Musketry Camp		150
	9	314

11TH BN "THE QUEEN'S" (R.W.S.) REGT

WEEKLY STRENGTH RETURN

	Killed		Wounded		Missing		Evacuated Sick		Struck off other purposes †		Officers notified struck off		Sent to Base		TOTAL Struck off		REINFORCEMENT		
	OFF	O.R	OFF	O.R	OFF	O.R	OFF	O.R	OFF	O.R	OFF	O.R	OFF	O.R	OFF	O.R	OFF	O.R	
SUNDAY 24th	—	1	—	11	—	—	—	—	—	—	—	—	—	—	—	12	1	5	1 November 13 3 " 22 " 23 " 24
MONDAY 25th	—	—	—	—	—	—	—	—	—	—	—	—	—	—	—	—	—	—	
TUESDAY 26th	—	—	—	—	—	—	—	—	—	—	—	—	—	—	—	—	—	—	
WEDNESDAY 27th	—	—	—	—	—	—	—	14	—	—	—	—	—	—	—	14	—	—	
THURSDAY 28th	—	—	—	—	—	—	—	—	—	—	—	—	—	—	—	—	—	—	
FRIDAY 29th	—	—	—	—	—	—	—	—	—	—	—	—	—	—	—	—	—	—	
SATURDAY 30th	—	1	—	11	—	—	—	14	—	—	—	—	—	—	—	26	—	5	

† Excludes those "slightly at duty"

DETAILS OVER.

	OFFICERS	O.R.
Strength last week	30	961
Deduct Struck off	—	26
Remaining	30	935
Add Reinforcements	—	5
Strength this week	30	940
	3	
		965

30th December 1916

R. Smith Capt for Lt Col.
Commanding 11th Bn The Queens (R.W.S.) Regt.

Nature of Work	Officers	O. R.
Attd Brigade & Div	2	27
" A. S. C.		2
Road Control		3
Divl Salvage	1	1
Intelligence		1
On Courses	2	39
Brigade Salvage		2
123rd T.M. Battery		16
1st Can. Tunnel Coy		6
250th Coy. R.E.		8
10th Corp. H.Q.		1
R.E. Corp Park		7
Divl Rest & F.A.	2	53
On leave		3
187th Bde R.F.A.		1
2nd Army School		1
Draft at Musketry Camp Instructors " " & Batman		153
	7	324

Army Form C. 2118

11 R W Surrey Rgt
Vol 9

WAR DIARY
or
INTELLIGENCE SUMMARY
(Erase heading not required.)

Instructions regarding War Diaries and Intelligence Summaries are contained in F.S. Regs., Part II. and the Staff Manual respectively. Title Pages will be prepared in manuscript.

Place	Date	Hour	Summary of Events and Information	Remarks and references to Appendices
			JANUARY 1917	
RENINGHELST	1st		In reserve billets.	
TRENCHES	2nd		Relieved 11th Royal West Kent Regt, in trenches – front line extending from O.3.a.q.o.10 canal at O.4.a.2.8. (Ref: Belgium Trench Map. WYSCHAETE. 28 S.W. 2. (Edition 3. D)	
RENINGHELST	7th		In reserve billets for training areas. (Relieved by 11th Royal West Kent Regt.)	
TRENCHES	14th 19th		Relieved 11th Royal West Kent Regt, in trenches, as above. On the night of 19th we raided enemy trenches, with Artillery co-operation, inflicting casualties & securing prisoner.	
RENINGHELST	21st		In reserve billets for training & rest. (Relieved by 11th Royal West Kent Regt.)	
TRENCHES	27th		Relieved 11th Royal West Kent Regt, in trenches, as above.	
			POSITION IN TRENCHES – Left flank of 41st Division. DIVISION ON OUR LEFT – 47th Division. SITUATION – Normal.	

January 31/17

[signature] Capt,
(commanding 11th (S) Bn. The Queen's (Royal West Surrey) Regt.

11th Bn "The Queen's" (R.W.S) Regt
Weekly Strength State

	KILLED		WOUNDED		MISSING		EVACUATED SICK		STRUCK OFF FOR OTHER PURPOSES		OFFICERS NOTIFIED STRUCK OFF		TOTAL STRUCK OFF		REINFORCEMENTS	
	OFF	OR	OFF	OR	OFF	OR	OFF	OR	OFF	OR	OFF	OR	OFF	OR	OFF	OR
SUNDAY 31st	—	—	—	1	—	—	—	—	—	—	—	1	—	1	—	4
MONDAY 1st	—	—	—	—	—	—	—	—	—	—	—	—	—	—	—	11
TUESDAY 2nd	—	—	—	—	—	1	—	—	—	—	—	1	—	1	1	—
WEDNESDAY 3rd	—	—	—	—	—	—	—	—	—	—	—	—	—	—	—	—
THURSDAY 4th	—	—	—	—	—	—	—	—	—	—	—	1	—	1	—	—
FRIDAY 5th	—	—	—	1	—	—	—	—	—	—	—	—	—	—	—	—
SATURDAY 6th	—	1	—	—	—	1	—	—	—	—	—	1	—	1	—	—
TOTAL	—	1	—	2	—	2	—	—	—	—	—	3	—	3	1	15

* Excludes those lightly off duty

DETAILS OVER

	OFF	OR
Strength last week	30	940
Deduct Struck off	1	3
Remaining	29	937
Add Reinforcements	1	15
Strength this week	30	952

January 4th 1917

A.J. Anderson 2/Lt
for Capt.
Cmdg. 11th Bn. The Queen's (R.W.S) Regt.

NATURE OF WORK.	Officers.	O.R.
Attached Brigade & Division.	3	26.
" A.S.C.		2.
Traffic Control		4.
Divisional Salvage	1	1.
Intelligence.		1.
On Courses.	2	48.
Brigade Salvage.		2.
123rd T.M.Bty.		16.
1st Can.Tunn.Coy.		6.
250th Coy. R.E.		8.
10th Corps H.Q.		2.
R.E.Corps Park.		7.
Divn. Rest & Field Ambulance.	1	50.
On Leave.		3.
187th Bde.R.F.A.		1.
2nd Army School.		1.
Draft & Instructors at Musketry Camp		152.
	7	330.

11th Bn "The Queens" (R.W.S.) Regt.

Weekly Strength Return

January	KILLED		WOUNDED		MISSING		EVACUATED SICK		STRUCK OFF FOR OTHER PURPOSES		SENT TO BASE		TOTAL STRUCK OFF		OFFICERS NOTIFIED STRUCK OFF	REINFORCEMENTS	
	OFF	OR	OFF	OR	OFF	OR	OFF	OR	OFF	OR	OFF	OR	OFF	OR	OFF	OFF	O.R.
Sunday 7th	-	-	-	2	-	-	-	-	-	-	-	-	-	2	-	-	-	2
Monday 8th	-	-	-	-	-	-	-	-	-	-	-	-	-	1	-	1	2	3
Tuesday 9th	-	-	-	-	-	-	-	2	-	-	-	-	-	2	-	-	2	1
Wednesday 10th	-	-	-	-	-	-	-	-	-	-	-	-	-	1	-	1	-	-
Thursday 11th	-	-	-	-	-	-	-	-	-	-	-	-	-	1	-	-	-	6
Friday 12th	-	-	-	-	-	-	-	-	-	1	-	-	-	1	-	1	-	-
Saturday 13th	-	-	-	-	-	-	-	-	-	-	1	-	1	-	-	-	-	-
TOTAL	-	-	-	2	-	-	-	2	-	1	1	-	1	4	-	3	-	11

* Excludes those slightly at duty.

	OFFICERS	O.R.
STRENGTH LAST WEEK	36	952
DEDUCT STRUCK OFF		4
REMAINING	30	948
ADD REINFORCEMENTS	3	11
STRENGTH THIS WEEK	33	959

DETAILS OVER

January 13th 1917

2/Lt
Capt
Comdg. 11th Bn "The Queens" (R.W.S. Reg)

Nature of Work	Officers	O.R.
Attached Bde & Division	3	27
" A.S.C.		2
Traffic Control		4
Divisional Salvage	1	1
Intelligence		1
On Courses	3	43
Brigade Salvage		2
123rd T.M. Battery		16
1st Can Tunnelling Coy		6
250th Coy. R.E.		8
10th Corps Hd. Qrs.		1
R.E. Corp Park		4
Divl. Rest & Field. A.	2	52
On Leave		1
187th Bde. R.F.A.		1
2nd Army School		1
Musketry Camp		14
At Étaples (Training for Commission)		1
123rd Bde School		77
	9	265

11th Bn "The Queen's" (R.W.S.) Regt.

Weekly Strength Return

	Killed		Wounded †		Missing		Evacuated Sick		Struck off for other purposes		Officers Notified Struck off	Sent to Base		Total Struck off		Reinforcements	
	OFF.	O.R.	OFF.	O.R.	OFF.	O.R.	OFF.	O.R.	OFF.	O.R.	OFF.	OFF.	O.R.	OFF.	O.R.	OFF.	O.R.
Sunday 14th																	
Monday 15th																1	-
Tuesday 16th		2		3											7		
Wednesday 17th																	
Thursday 18th								2									
Friday 19th																	
Saturday 20th																	
TOTAL		2		3				2							7	1	-

† Excludes those "Slightly at duty"

DETAILS OVER

	OFFICERS	O.R.
Strength last week	33	959
Deduct Struck off		7
Remaining	33	952
Add Reinforcements	1	-
Strength this week	34	952
	1 M.G.	30 R.E. as
	1 Capt.	12 T.M.B.
	36	967

20th January 1917

[signature] A.B.V. [?]
O.C. Commanding 11th Bn "The Queen's" (R.W.S.) Regt.

2/Lt. for O.C.
11th Bn "The Queen's" (R.W.S.) Regt.

NATURE OF WORK.	Officers.	O.R.
Attd. Bde. & Divn.	4.	27.
" A. S. C.		2.
Traffic Control.		4.
Div. Salvage.	1	1.
Intelligence		1.
On Courses	4	49.
Brigade Salvage.		2.
123rd T.M. Battery.		16.
1st Canadian Tunn. Coy.		6.
250th Coy. R. E.		8.
R.E. Corps Park		7.
10th Corps. Hd. Qrs.		1.
Divisional Rest & Field Ambulance.	2	71.
On Leave	1	1.
187th Bde. R. F. A.		1.
2nd Army School		1.
Musketry School.	1	22.
At Etaples (Training for Commission)		1.
123rd Bde. School.	3	78.
	16.	299

11th Bn "The Queen's" (R.W.S.) Regt

WEEKLY STRENGTH RETURN

JANUARY	KILLED		WOUNDED		MISSING		EVACUATED SICK		STRUCK OFF For OTHER PURPOSES		OFFICERS NOTIFIED STRUCK OFF		SENT TO BASE		TOTAL STRUCK OFF		REINFORCEMENTS	
	OFF	O.R	OFF	O.R	OFF	O.R	OFF	O.R	OFF	O.R	OFF	O.R	OFF	O.R	OFF	O.R	OFF	O.R
SUNDAY 21st	-	-	2	-	-	1	-	-	-	4	-	-	-	-	-	12	-	4
MONDAY 22nd	-	-	-	-	-	-	-	3	-	-	-	-	-	-	-	3	3	134
TUESDAY 23rd	-	-	-	-	-	-	-	-	-	-	-	-	-	-	-	-	-	-
WEDNESDAY 24th	-	-	-	-	-	-	-	-	-	-	-	-	-	-	-	-	-	-
THURSDAY 25th	-	-	-	-	-	-	-	-	-	-	-	-	-	-	-	-	-	-
FRIDAY 26th	-	-	-	-	-	-	-	-	-	-	-	-	-	1	-	1	-	-
SATURDAY 27th	-	2	-	9	-	1	-	3	-	1	-	-	-	-	-	15	3	138

wounded thro' enemy act'y.

	OFF	O.R
Strength last week		
Deduct struck off		
Reinforcements		
Add Reinforcement		
Strength this week		

27th January 1917

Commanding 11th Bn "The Queen's" Regt

2/Lt. for Syphilis

NATURE OF WORK.	OFFICERS.	O.R.
Attd. Bde. & Divn.	5	28.
" A. S. C.		2.
Traffic Control.		4.
Div. Salvage.	1	1.
Intelligence		1.
On Courses.	3	48.
Brigade Salvage.		2.
123rd T.M.Bty.		16.
1st. Can. Tunn. Coy.		6.
250th Coy. R.E.		8.
R.E. Corps Park.		7
10th Corps. H.Q.		1.
Divisional Rest & Field Ambulance	5	74.
On Leave		1.
187th Bde. R.F.A.		1.
2nd Army School	2	151.
Perm. Drainage Party.		19.
Etaples (Training for Commission).		1.
	16.	372.

11th Queens R.West Surrey Regt
for the Month of February 1917
Vol 10

Army Form C. 2118

WAR DIARY
or
INTELLIGENCE SUMMARY

(Erase heading not required.)

Place	Date	Hour	Summary of Events and Information	Remarks and references to Appendices
In the Field	1/2/17	1 a.m.	On this date the 11th Battalion "The Queens" Royal West Surrey Regt. were in garrison in trenches - the front line extending from O.3.c.4.7 to O.4.a.2.8. (Ref. Trench map Ypres-Comines Canal at O.U.a.2.8. S.W.2). WYTSCHAETE. 28. S.W. 2).	
"	2/2/17		The 11th Queen's Royal West Surrey Regt, was relieved in the above trenches by the 11th Bn Royal West Kent Regt, & returned to camp at RENINGHELST for rest & training.	
"	9/2/17		The 11th Queens Royal West Surrey Regt, returned to trenches & relieved the 11th Royal West Kent Regt. The situation was quiet during the relief.	
	9/2/17 to 16/2/17		Situation quiet, with intermittent artillery activity. Casualties sustained during this tour were six O.R. wounded, + one O.R. killed	
	16/2/17		The 11th Queens Royal West Surrey Regt, was relieved on this date by the 11th Bn. Royal West Kent Regt, & returned to camp at RENINGHELST for rest & training.	
	21/2/17		The 11th Queens Royal West Surrey Regt, returned to the trenches & relieved the 11th Royal West Kent Regt. The relief was carried out under normal conditions.	
	21/2/17 to 26/2/17		During this period in garrison in the above trenches - the conditions were normal with slightly increased artillery activity. Casualties sustained were - One officer & two O.R. wounded.	
	24/2/17		At 5.15 p.m. on this date the 10th Queens raided enemy trenches opposite the right of our Divisional Front. As a precaution against retaliation we withdrew from our front line leaving Lewis Gunners & Snipers, & scouts in Suffolk Trenches. We only sustained one casualty during the ensuing bombardment. (over)	

Army Form C. 2118

WAR DIARY
or
INTELLIGENCE SUMMARY
(Erase heading not required.)

Instructions regarding War Diaries and Intelligence Summaries are contained in F. S. Regs., Part II. and the Staff Manual respectively. Title Pages will be prepared in manuscript.

Place	Date	Hour	Summary of Events and Information	Remarks and references to Appendices
In the Field	26/2/17		On this date the 11th Bn. Royal West Surrey Regt. was relieved in trenches by the 11th Bn. Royal West Kent Regt. & returned to camp at RENINGHELST for rest + training. General Notes.— Position occupied in trenches — Left flank of Left Brigade (123rd) of the 41st Division. Division on our left — — — — the 47th Division. The general situation has been quiet. The enemy's retaliation to our continual harassing has not been severe.	

R. Otter Lt. Col.
Commanding, the 11th (S) Bn. the Queen's (Royal West Surrey) Regt.
1st March 1917.

11th Bn The Queen's (R.W.S.) Regt.

Weekly Strength Return

JANUARY & FEBRUARY	KILLED		WOUNDED *		MISSING		EVACUATED SICK		STRUCK OFF FOR OTHER PURPOSES		OFFICERS NOTIFIED STRUCK OFF	SENT TO BASE		TOTAL STRUCK OFF		REINFORCEMENTS		
	OFF	O.R.	OFF	O.R.	OFF	O.R.	OFF	O.R.	OFF	O.R.	OFF	OFF	O.R.	OFF	O.R.	OFF	O.R.	OR
SUNDAY 28th	—	1	1	1(2)/(5½)	1	1	1(1sck)(2sck)/5¼(sck)(1sck)	—	—	—	—	—	1	2	9	—	1	
MONDAY 29th	—	3	—	1	—	1	—	1(sck)/1(sck)	—	—	—	—	1	—	4	—	1	
TUESDAY 30th	—	1	—	1	—	1	—	1(sck)/1(sck)	—	—	—	—	1	1	1	—	2	
WEDNESDAY 31st	—	1	—	1	—	1	—	1	—	—	—	—	1	—	1	—	1	
THURSDAY 1st	—	1	—	1	—	1	—	1	—	—	—	—	1	1	1	1	1	
FRIDAY 2nd	—	1	—	1	—	1	—	1	—	—	—	—	1	—	1	—	1	1
SATURDAY 3rd	—	3	—	2	—	1	—	8	—	1	—	—	1	2	13	2	2	1

* Evacuated Sick to Duty

DETAILS
OVER

Strength Last Week
Deduct Struck Off
Remaining
Add Reinforcements
Strength this Week

	Officers	O.R.
	38	1075
	3½	1062
	36	1063
	1	7
	39	1069

3rd February 1917

Commanding 11th Bn. The Queen's (R.W.S.) Regt.

Nature of Work.	Officers	O.R
Attached Bde Hqrs	5	29
A.S.C.		2
Traffic Control		4
Gov Salvage	1	1
Intelligence		1
On Courses	3	60
Brigade Salvage		1
123rd T.M. Battery		16
1st Canadian Tunn. Coy.		6
250th Coy. R.E.		8
R.E. Corps Park		7
10th " Hd Qrs		1
Divisional Reser. Field Ambulance	4	72
On Leave	1	
184th Bde R.F.A.		1
2nd Army School		1
River Drainage Party		19
Musketry School	1	148
At Etaples Training for Commission		1
	15	378

11th BN. "The Queen's" (R.W.S.) Regiment

WEEKLY STRENGTH RETURN

FEBRUARY	KILLED *		WOUNDED		MISSING		EVACUATED SICK		STRUCK OFF FOR OTHER PURPOSES		OFFICERS NOTIFIED STRUCK OFF	SENT TO BASE		TOTAL STRUCK OFF		REINFORCEMENTS	
	OFF.	O.R.	OFF.	O.R.	OFF.	O.R.	OFF.	O.R.	OFF.	O.R.	OFF.	OFF.	O.R.	OFF.	O.R.	OFF.	O.R.
SUNDAY 4th								23-1-17 1									
MONDAY 5th																1	
TUESDAY 6th																	
WEDNESDAY 7th																	
THURSDAY 8th																	
FRIDAY 9th																	
SATURDAY 10th								1								1	

* Excludes those "Slightly at duty"

DETAILS OVER	OFFICERS	O.R.
STRENGTH LAST WEEK	36	1087
DEDUCT STRUCK OFF		
REMAINING	36	1080
ADD REINFORCEMENTS	1	
STRENGTH THIS WEEK	37	1080

W. Winterbury
2/Lt a/Adjt for Coot.
Commanding 11th Bn "The Queen's" (R.W.S.) Regt.

11th February 1917

NATURE OF WORK.	Officers.	O.R.
Attd. Bds. & Divn.	5	32.
" A.S.C.		2.
Traffic Control.		4.
Div. Salvage.	1	1.
Intelligence.		1.
Bde. Salvage.		2.
On Courses.	3	73.
123rd T.M. Bty.		16.
1st. Can. Tunn. Coy.		6.
250th Coy. R.E.		8.
R.E. Corps Park.		7.
10th Corps H.Q.		1.
Div. Rest & Field Ambulance.	6	82.
On Leave.	1	2.
187th Bde. R.F.A.		1.
2nd Army School.		1.
Perm. Drainage Party.		19.
Musketry School.	1	148.
At Etaples Training for Commission.		1.
	17.	406.

11TH BN. "THE QUEEN'S" (R.W.S.) REGT.

WEEKLY STRENGTH RETURN.

FEBRUARY		KILLED		WOUNDED ✕		MISSING		EVACUATED SICK		STRUCK OFF FOR OTHER PURPOSES		OFFICERS NOTIFIED STRUCK OFF.	SENT TO BASE		TOTAL STRUCK OFF.		REINFORCEMENTS			
		OFF.	O.R.	OFF.	O.R.	OFF.	O.R.	OFF.	O.R.	OFF.	O.R.	OFF.	OFF.	O.R.	OFF.	O.R.	OFF.	O.R.		
SUNDAY	11th	-	1 (9-2-17)	-	2 (9-2-17)(10-2-17)	-	-	-	-	-	5	-	-	-	-	9	-	-		
MONDAY	12th	-	-	-	1	-	-	-	-	-	-	-	-	-	-	1	1	1		
TUESDAY	13th	-	-	-	1	-	-	-	-	-	-	-	-	-	-	1	-	1		
WEDNESDAY	14th	-	-	-	1	-	-	-	-	-	-	-	-	-	-	1	-	-		
THURSDAY	15th	-	-	-	1	-	-	-	-	1	-	-	-	-	1	1	-	-		
FRIDAY	16th	-	-	-	-	-	-	-	-	-	-	-	-	-	-	-	-	-		
SATURDAY	17th	-	1	-	7	-	-	-	-	1	5	-	-	-	1	13	1	1		

※ EXCLUDES THOSE "SLIGHTLY AT DUTY"

DETAILS OVER.

	OFF.	O.R.
STRENGTH LAST WEEK	37	1080
DEDUCT STRUCK OFF	1	13
REMAINING	36	1067
ADD REINFORCEMENTS	1	1
STRENGTH THIS WEEK	37	1068

17th 3 O.R.C.Bn
1 M.B.

16 FEBRUARY 1917

Act. Adj. for Capt.
Commanding 11th Bn "The Queen's" (R.W.S.) Regt.

21 Lieut.

NATURE OF WORK.	OFFICERS.	O. R.
Attd. Bde & Divn.	2.	32.
" A.S.C.		2.
Traffic Control.		4.
Div. Salvage.	1	1.
Intelligence		1.
Brigade Salvage		2.
On Courses.	6	40.
123rd T.M.Bty.		17.
" M.G.Coy.		4.
1st. Can. Tunn. Coy.		6.
Perm. Drainage Party.		19.
250th Coy. R.E.		8.
R.E. Corps Park.		7.
10th Corps H.Q.		1.
Div. Rest & Field Ambulance	9	87.
On Leave.	1	2.
2 nd Army School.		1.
Musketry School.		26.
At Etaples (Training for Commission).		1.
	20.	261.

1st Bn. THE QUEEN'S (R.W.S.) REGT.

WEEKLY STRENGTH RETURN

FEBRUARY	KILLED			MISSING		EVACUATED SICK		STRUCK OFF FOR OTHER PURPOSES		OFFICERS NOTIFIED STRUCK O.FF.		OFFICERS SENT TO BASE		TOTAL STRUCK OFF.		REINFORCEMENTS		REINFORCEMENTS
	OFF	O.R		OFF	O.R	OFF	O.R	OFF	O.R	OFF	O.R	OFF	O.R	OFF	O.R	OFF	O.R	O.R
SUNDAY 18th	-	-		-	-	-	5	-	-	-	1	-	1	-	5	1/2-17/2-17	5	-
MONDAY 19th	-	-		-	-	-	-	-	-	-	-	-	-	-	-	-	-	-
TUESDAY 20th	-	-		-	-	-	-	-	-	-	-	-	-	-	-	3	4	-
WEDNESDAY 21st	-	-		-	-	-	-	-	-	-	-	-	-	-	-	-	-	-
THURSDAY 22nd	-	-		-	1	-	-	-	-	-	-	-	-	-	1	-	-	-
FRIDAY 23rd	-	-		-	-	-	-	-	-	-	-	-	-	-	-	-	-	-
SATURDAY 24th	-	-		-	1	-	5	-	-	-	-	-	-	-	6	5	9	-

DETAILS
STRENGTH LAST WEEK 37 1011
DED. NUMBER STRUCK OFF 6
REMAINING 37 1005
ADD REINFORCEMENTS 5 9
STRENGTH THIS WEEK 42 1014

VILLAGES FREE LIGHT DUTY
OFF. O.R

24th February 1917

[signature]
Lieutenant Colonel
Commanding 1st Bn. The Queen's (R.W.S.) Regt.

Act. Adjt. Lt.
2nd Lieut.
Act. Adjt. 1st Bn. The Queen's (R.W.S.) Regt.

NATURE OF WORK.	OFFICERS.	O.R.
Attd. Bde & Divn.	2	31.
" A.S.C.		2.
Traffic Control.		4.
Div. Salvage.	1	1.
Intelligence		1.
Brigade Salvage.		2.
On Courses.	3	56.
123rd T.M.Bty.		17.
" M.G.Coy.		6.
1st. Can. Tunn. Coy.		6.
Perm. Drainage Party.		18.
250th Coy. R.E.		8.
R.E. Corps Park.		6.
10th Corps H.Q.	1	2.
Div. Rest & Field Ambulance.	9	102.
On Leave.	1	1.
2nd Army School.		5.
Musketry School.		22.
Etaples.		4.
No. 33 Prisoners of War Camp.	1	1.
Draft at Steenvoorde.	1	117.
	19.	412.

WAR DIARY

11th Queens Royal West Surrey Regt.

Army Form C. 2118

INTELLIGENCE SUMMARY ~~or~~ for the Month of MARCH 1917

(Erase heading not required.)

Instructions regarding War Diaries and Intelligence Summaries are contained in F.S. Regs., Part II. and the Staff Manual respectively. Title Pages will be prepared in manuscript.

Place	Date	Hour	Summary of Events and Information	Remarks and references to Appendices
RENINGHELST	1/3/17	12 a.m.	On this date the Battalion was resting at ALBERTA CAMP (nr Jolt's) for rest and training. —	
SPOIL BANK (B.H.Q.) I.33.a.0.6	4/3/17	6 p.m.	Relieved the 11th Battalion Royal West Kent Regt and garrisoned Trenches O.32, O.33, O.34, O.35, O.36, O.37, O.38, at O.41, the front line of which extends from O.3.c.8.9 to the YPRES-COMINES CANAL at O.4.a.2½.8. Reference:- TRENCH MAP — WYTSCHAETE 28. S.W. 2. 1/10,000. The conditions were very quiet during this period. Lieut. J. MAHONY (wounded on 24/2/17) four — Casualties — 1 O.R. wounded. 1 O.R. died on this date.	TRENCH STRENGTH 19 Officers & 569 O.Rs. TOTAL STRENGTH 42 Officers & 1058 O.Rs.
"	10/3/17	"	Relieved by the 11th Battalion Royal West Kent Regt and returned to the Jolt's at ALBERTA CAMP for rest and training. —	
"	16/3/17	"	Proceeded to the trenches as above and relieved the 11th Battalion Royal West Kent Regiment. Conditions again quiet and Casualties 3 O.R. wounded. —	TRENCH STRENGTH 15 Officers & 586 O.Rs. TOTAL STRENGTH 39 Officers & 1045 O.Rs.
"	22/3/17	"	Relieved by the 11th Bn Royal West Kent Regt, and returned to the Jolt's at ALBERTA CAMP for rest and training. —	
"	24/3/17	4.30 p.m. to 7.30 p.m.	On this date the Enemy bombarded and attempted to raid our trenches particularly in the vicinity of O.41. then garrisoned by the 11th Bn Royal West Kent Regiment and were repulsed. During this period the Battalion were ordered to 'stand to' which in	

WAR DIARY
INTELLIGENCE SUMMARY

Army Form C. 2118

Place	Date	Hour	Summary of Events and Information	Remarks and references to Appendices
Camp nr ALBERTA	March 24th	12 p.m.	On this date the Battalion after Church Parade proceeded to CHIPPEWA (the training ground of the 23rd Middlesex Regiment) when Medal Ribbons were presented at M.A.6.central) by the Divisional General, Major General S.T.B. LAWFORD. C.B. The following Officers, N.C.O's & man of the Battalion received presentation of Medal Ribbons from the General:- 1. CAPT. E.G. BOWDEN — MILITARY CROSS 2. 2 Lt. A.E. RYAN — " Nº. G. 11151. L/Sgt. W. de COURCY — MILITARY MEDAL " G. 11685. L/Sgt. G.M. SYER — " " G. 1176. Private F.S.M. MORLEY — "	TRENCH STRENGTH: 17 officers 540 O.Rs Total Strength 41 officers 1022 O.Rs
SPOIL BANK	29/3/17	7 p.m.	On this date the Battalion relieved the 11th Bn Royal West Kent Regt & took over the Trenches as above. Conditions again general. During the periods the Battalion was in the Trenches Casualties NIL. The RIGHT Battalion of the 47th Division was on the LEFT of the Battalion & the 10th R.W. Kent Regt of 23rd Middlesex on the RIGHT. P. Otter Lieut. Col: Commanding 11th Bn "The Queens" (R.W.S.) Regt 30th March 1917.	

11th Bn. The Queen's (RWS) Regt.

WEEKLY STRENGTH RETURN

February/March	KILLED		WOUNDED		MISSING		EVACUATED SICK		STRUCK OFF FOR OTHER PURPOSES		OFFICERS NOTIFIED STRUCK OFF	SENT TO BASE		TOTAL STRUCK OFF		REINFORCEMENTS	
	OFF	O.R.	OFF	O.R.	OFF	O.R.	OFF	O.R.	OFF	O.R.	OFFICERS	OFF	O.R.	OFF	O.R.	OFF	O.R.
SUNDAY 25	-	1	2/off 1 off	1	-	-	-	2/off 1	-	1	-	-	-	-	1	1	4
MONDAY 26	-	1	1	2	-	-	-	2/off 1	-	4/off 2	-	-	-	-	-	-	14
TUESDAY 27	-	1	1	-	-	-	-	1	-	-	-	-	-	-	-	-	3
WEDNESDAY 30	-	1	1	-	-	-	-	1 off 1	-	-	-	-	-	-	-	-	-
THURSDAY 1	-	1	1	-	-	-	-	1 off 1	-	1	-	-	-	-	-	-	-
FRIDAY 2	-	1	1	-	-	-	-	1 off 1	-	-	-	-	-	-	-	-	-
SATURDAY 3	-	1	1	2	-	-	-	8	-	4	-	-	-	-	16	1	3

DETAILS OVER

3 March. 1917

	OFF	O.R.
STRENGTH LAST WEEK	42	1071
DEDUCT STRUCK OFF	-	16
REMAINING	42	1055
ADD REINFORCEMENTS	1	3
STRENGTH THIS WEEK	43	1058

A.B.Whint(?)
Lt Col.
Commdg 11th Bn. The Queen's Regt.

Nature of Work	Officers	O.R.
Attchd Bde & Div.	2	54
" A.S.C.		2
Traffic Control		4
Divl Salvage	1	1
Intelligence		1
On Course	4	64
Bde Salvage		1
123rd T.M.B.		17
1st Canadian Tunn. Coy.		6
250th R.E.		8
R.E. Corps Park		6
10th " H.Q.	4	14
Divl Rest & Field Ambulance etc	7	90
On Leave		
187th Bde R.F.A.		1
2nd Army School		21
Firm Drainage Party		19
Musketry School		22
On Command Etaples	1	
123 M.G. Coy.		5
	19	327

11th (S) Bn. "The Queen's"/R.W.S. Regt.

WEEKLY STRENGTH RETURN

March	KILLED		WOUNDED*		MISSING		EVACUATED SICK		STRUCK OFF FOR OTHER PURPOSES		OFFICERS NOTIFIED STRUCK OFF		SENT TO BASE		TOTAL STRUCK OFF		REINFORCEMENTS	
	OFF	OR	OFF	OR	OFF	OR	OFF	OR	OFF	OR	OFF	OR	OFF	OR	OFF	OR	OFF	OR
SUNDAY 4th	-	-	-	-	-	-	-	4-2-17 1	-	-	-	-	-	-	-	-	-	1
MONDAY 5th	-	1	-	-	-	-	-	2-3-17 1	-	2	-	-	-	1	-	2	-	1
TUESDAY 6th	-	-	-	-	-	-	-	-	-	-	-	-	-	-	-	-	-	1
WEDNESDAY 7th	-	-	-	1	-	-	-	13-2-17 2	-	-	-	-	-	-	-	1	-	-
THURSDAY 8th	-	-	-	-	-	-	-	16-2-17 2	-	-	-	-	7	-	-	10	-	3
FRIDAY 9th	-	-	-	-	-	-	-	16-2-17 2	-	-	-	-	-	-	-	1	-	1
SATURDAY 10th	-	1	-	-	-	-	-	1	-	-	-	-	-	-	-	-	-	-
TOTAL	-	1	-	1	-	-	-	8	-	2	-	-	-	1	-	13	-	3

*Excludes those "Slightly at Duty"

	OFF	OR
STRENGTH LAST WEEK	43	1034
DEDUCT STRUCK OFF		13
REMAINING	43	1043
ADD REINFORCEMENTS		3
STRENGTH THIS WEEK	43	1046

10th March 1917

[signature]
2/Lt & act Adjt
for Lt Col
Commdg 11th(S) Bn "The Queen's" (R.W.S) Regt.

Nature of Work.	Officers	O.R.
Attached Brigade and Division.	1	37.
" A.S.C.		2.
Traffic Control		4.
Divisional Salvage	1	1.
Intelligence		1.
On Course	4	55.
Brigade Salvage		1.
183rd. T.M.B.		17.
250 R.E. & 232 R.E.		13.
R.E. Corps Park		6.
Xth. Corps H.Q. & Training Camp.	5	40.
Div. Rest & F.A. etc.	7	90.
2nd. Army School.		4.
Permanent Drainage Party.		19.
Musketry School		13.
On Command & Etaples	1	5.
123rd. M.G. Coy.		6.
Total.	19	314.

11th/13th "The Queen's" (R.W.S.) Regt.

WEEKLY STRENGTH STATE

MARCH	KILLED OFF	KILLED O.R	WOUNDED OFF	WOUNDED O.R	MISSING OFF	MISSING O.R	EVACUATED SICK OFF	EVACUATED SICK O.R	STRUCK OFF OTHER PURPOSES OFF	STRUCK OFF OTHER PURPOSES O.R	OFFICERS STRUCK OFF OFF	SENT TO BASE OFF	SENT TO BASE O.R	TOTAL STRUCK OFF OFF	TOTAL STRUCK OFF O.R	REINFORCEMENTS OFF	REINFORCEMENTS O.R
SUNDAY 11th	-	-	-	-	-	-	1	5	+2	+7 x.3.17	-	-	1	3	6	1	11
MONDAY 12th	-	-	-	-	-	-	-	-	-	1	-	-	-	-	1	-	11
TUESDAY 13th	-	-	-	-	-	-	-	-	-	-	-	-	-	-	-	-	-
WEDNESDAY 14th	-	-	-	-	-	-	-	-	-	-	-	-	1	1	1	-	-
THURSDAY 15th	-	-	-	-	-	-	-	-	-	-	-	-	1	1	1	-	-
FRIDAY 16th	-	-	-	-	-	-	-	-	-	-	-	-	1	-	1	1	-
SATURDAY 17th	-	-	-	-	-	-	1	-	2	2	-	-	1	3	7	1	4

X Excludes those "Slightly at Duty"

	OFFICERS	O.R
Strength last week	43	1045
Deduct struck off	3	7
Reinforcement	40	1038
Add Reinforcements	-	4
Strength this week	40	1045

17th March 1917

[signature]

O.C. 11th Bn. The Queen's Regt.

1/c of Adje
for Lt. Col.
Comdg 11th Bn the Queen's Regt.

Nature of Work.	Officers	O.R.
Attached Brigade & Division.	1	39
" A.S.C.		2
Traffic Control.		4
Divisional Salvage	1	1.
Intelligence		1.
On Courses	7	66.
Brigade Salvage		1.
123rd. T. M. B.		21.
350th. R.E. & 338rd. R.E.		14.
R.E. Corps Park.		6.
Xth. Corps H. Q., Training Camp etc.	3	7.
Div. Rest & P. A. etc.	7	74.
2nd. Army School.		4.
Permanent Drainage Party.		10.
Musketry School.		13.
On Command & Etaples.	1	3.
123rd. M. G. Coy.		6.
Attached A. V. C.		1.
1st. Canadian Tunn. Coy.		39.
R.C.E.		11.
Leave		1.
	19	309.

11th Bn. "The Queen's" (R.W.S.) Regt.

WEEKLY STRENGTH RETURN.

MARCH.	KILLED		WOUNDED		MISSING		EVACUATED SICK		STRUCK OFF FOR OTHER PURPOSES		OFFICERS NOTIFIED STRUCK OFF	SENT TO BASE		TOTAL STRUCK OFF		REINFORCEMENTS	
	OFF.	O.R.	OFF.	O.R.	OFF.	O.R.	OFF.	O.R.	OFF.	O.R.	OFFRS.	OFF.	O.R.	OFF.	O.R.	OFFRS	O.R.
SUNDAY. 18th	-	-	-	1	-	-	-	17-3-17 3	-	-	-	-	-	-	4	1	1
MONDAY 19th	-	-	-	1	-	-	1	4	-	1	1	-	-	1	9	1	-
TUESDAY 20th	-	-	-	-	-	-	-	2	-	-	-	-	-	-	2	-	-
WEDNESDAY 21st	-	-	-	1	-	-	-	-	-	-	-	-	-	-	1	1	-
THURSDAY 22nd	-	-	-	-	-	-	-	2	-	1	-	-	-	-	1	-	-
FRIDAY 23rd	-	-	-	-	-	-	-	-	-	2	-	-	-	-	2	-	-
SATURDAY 24th	1	-	-	3	-	-	1	1† 4	-	9	-	-	-	1	20	1	2

† Excludes those "Slightly at Duty".

	OFFRS.	O.R.
STRENGTH LAST WEEK.	39	1043
DEDUCT STRUCK OFF	1	20
REMAINING.	38	1023
ADD REINFORCEMENTS.	1	3
STRENGTH THIS WEEK	39	1026

24th March 1917

Lt. & Adjutant

for Major
Commanding 11th (S) Bn. "The Queen's" (R.W.S.) Regt.

NATURE OF WORK	OFF	O.R.
Att'ch'd Bde & Divn.	1	36
" A.S.C		2
Traffic Control		3
Divl Salvage	1	1
Intelligence		1
On Course	9	52
Bde Salvage		1
123 T.M.B.		19
250th RE		8
233rd RE		7
R E Corps Park		6
Xth Corps HQ	1	2
Div Rest & T.S. Rect.	6	70
2nd Army School		3
On Command & Etaples	1	6
123rd M.G. Coy.		6
Att'ch'd A.V.C		1
1 Canr. Limm. Coy.		28
R.C.E.		11
Leave		1
Permanent Drainage Party		19
Musketry Schl		14
Total	19	298

11th Bn "The Queen's" (R.W.S.) Regt.

WEEKLY STRENGTH RETURN

	Killed		Wounded #		Missing		Evacuated Sick		Struck off other than performance		Officers notified struck off	Sent to Base		Total Struck off		Reinforcements	
	OFF.	O.R.	OFF.	O.R.	OFF.	O.R.	OFF.	O.R.	OFF.	O.R.	OFFICERS	OFF.	O.R.	OFF.	O.R.	OFF.	O.R.
SUNDAY 25th	-	-	-	-	-	-	-	11	-	-	-	-	-	1	11	1	25-3R
MONDAY 26th	-	-	-	1	-	-	-	-	-	-	-	-	-	-	1	1	1
TUESDAY 27th	-	-	-	-	-	-	-	-	-	-	-	-	-	-	-	-	5
WEDNESDAY 28th	-	-	-	-	-	-	-	-	-	-	-	-	-	-	1	1	-
THURSDAY 29th	-	-	-	-	-	-	-	-	-	-	-	-	-	-	-	-	-
FRIDAY 30th	-	-	-	-	-	-	-	-	-	-	-	-	1	-	-	1	-
SATURDAY 31st	1	-	1	-	-	-	1	11	-	-	-	-	-	1	12	3	7

\# Excludes those "Slightly at duty"

DETAILS.
OVER.

	OFFICERS	O.R.
Strength last week	39	1027
Deaths & Losses off	1	12
Remaining	38	1015
add Reinforcements	3	7
Strength this week	41	1022

31st March 1917

A.B. Wroten
Actg Adjt for
Comndg. 11th Bn "The Queen's" (R.W.S.) Regt.
Lt. Col.

	Officers	O.R.
2nd Army Schl of Instructions.	—	—
Xth Corps Hd. Qrs. (Includes 1 Servant)	7	1
Divisnl Employ. (" " ")	1	10
Brigade " (" 2 Servts, 1 Salvage + 1 Transport.		19.
Attchd. A.S.C. (Loaders)		2
" Brigade Hd. Qrs. (" 1 Servant)	1	7.
" 123 M.G.C.		6
" " L.T.M. Bty.		14
" Divl Tunn. Coy.		5
" 1st. Cana. Tunn Coy.		28
" R.C.E.		11
" G.H.Q.		1
2nd Army Musketry School		5
233rd Coy R.E.		9
Xth Corps R.E. Park.		6
Courses.	9	81
Field Amb, Divl Rstete.	4	69
Traffic Control		4
Waples.		2
Permanent Drainage Party		19
Y.M.C.A		1
Xth Corps Training Camp.		—
33rd Prisoners of War Camp	1	1
Div Command	1	3
2nd Army Purchase Board		2
Attached A.V.C.		1
Total	17	299

WAR DIARY
or
INTELLIGENCE SUMMARY
(Erase heading not required.)

Army Form C. 2118

XI R.W.Surrey Regt

Set 72

Place	Date	Hour	Summary of Events and Information	Remarks and references to Appendices
	1.4.17		In the trenches – Left Sector of 41st Division. Front line of Battalion Sector extending from O3.c.6.8. to the YPRES – COMINES CANAL at O4.a.2.8. (Ref. Trench Map. WYTSCHAETE. 28 SW.2.)	
	4.4.17		Relieved by the 11th Royal West Kent Regt, & proceeded to huts at RENINGHELST. The Tour in trenches was quiet.	
	6.4.17		Left RENINGHELST & marched to STEENVOORDE en route for training area at HOULLE.	
	7.4.17		Marched from STEENVOORDE to NOORDPEENE.	
	8.4.17		Marched from NOORDPEENE to HOULLE.	
	10.4.17 to		At HOULLE for rest & training. Special training in attack.	
	22.4.17			
	23.4.17		Left HOULLE & marched to NOORDPEENE en route for RENINGHELST.	
	24.4.17		Marched from NOORDPEENE to STEENVOORDE.	
	25.4.17		Marched from STEENVOORDE to RENINGHELST.	
	26.4.17 to 30.4.17		Battalion occupied in Working Parties & continuation of training.	

May 2nd 1917.

R. Oter Lt. Col.
Commanding – 11th Queen's (Royal West Surrey) Regt.,

WAR DIARY or INTELLIGENCE SUMMARY

Army Form C. 2118

MAY 1917 1/13 1/7(S) Bn "THE QUEEN'S REGT."

Place	Date	Hour	Summary of Events and Information	Remarks and references to Appendices
RENNINGHELST	1/5/17	—	In rest. Killed at RENNINGHELST 9.11.7 C.S.M (a/R.S.M) Higgins wounded "Croix de Guerre." Bad. Yag. 1.5.17.	
In the line	3/5/17	—	Relieved 10th Bn "The Queen's Regt." in Support near VOORMEZEELE (Map 28 N.W.) During tour had 1 O.R. killed and 5 O.R. wounded.	
In the line	7/5/17	—	Relieved 10th Bn. Royal W. Kent Regt. in front line & supports from O.2c.9.8 to O.3.L.2.2. (Map at 28.S.W.2.E/10,000). Enemy artillery active during this tour. Had 1 off. wounded, 3 O.R. killed and 5 O.R. wounded.	
RENNINGHELST	14/5/17	—	Relieved by K.R.R.s in the line, went back into billets at RENNINGHELST for rest & training. 9.11.17 C.S.M Elts. F.C. 911607/4/Gl Martin 341 & 13.419, Pte Japp. 27 mentioned in dispatches 9/4/17.	
In the line	26.5.17	—	Relieved 15th Bn. Hants Regt. in support near VOORMEZEELE. Enemy artillery much more active in retaliation for our bombardments. Had 2 O.R. killed, 6 wounded and 3 wounded (slightly at duty). Relieved by 12th Bn. East Surrey Regt. in support. Went back to RENNINGHELST	
RENNINGHELST	31.5.17		for rest and training. Left Battalion at 123rd B.de, 41st Div. On our left - 47th Div.	

Harry Maddock, Major
for Lt. Col. Commanding
1/7 (S) Bn. The Queen's Regt.

WAR DIARY or INTELLIGENCE SUMMARY

Army Form C. 2118

War Diary.

11th [S] Bn "The Queen's" (R.W.S.) Regt.

June 1st – 30th 1917.

WAR DIARY
or
INTELLIGENCE SUMMARY
(Erase heading not required.)

Army Form C. 2118

Instructions regarding War Diaries and Intelligence Summaries are contained in F.S. Regs., Part II. and the Staff Manual respectively. Title Pages will be prepared in manuscript.

Place	Date 1917 JUNE	Hour	Summary of Events and Information	Remarks and references to Appendices
RENINGHELST BELGIUM	1ST 2ND 3RD 4TH 5TH		Battⁿ in training at Reninghelst.	MAP SHEET 28 SWA. APPENDIX I Operation Orders. APPENDIX II MAP. 2ND ARMY.
Sheet 28 SW2. O 3 a 7 9½	6TH	12 MN	At 12 Midnight of night June 5-6 the Battⁿ marched by Companies from ALBERTA CAMP, RENINGHELST to the Assembly area where it occupied a position in OLD FRENCH TRENCH at O 3 a 7 9½. Strength of Battⁿ in the line was 17 Officers + 550 ORs. Major Wardell was in Command in the absence of Lt Col Otter - sick.	
	7TH	12.30AM	At 12.30AM night 6-7 June the Battⁿ moved on to tapes laid out behind our front line between O 3 c 15.75 and O 3 b 40.20; a front of about 220 yards. The right flank was on the right of the MUD PATCH + the left on the left of TRIANGULAR WOOD. On the right was the 10TH R.W.K. Regt + on the left the 8TH Bⁿ LONDON REGT. (47TH DIVN). In support - 20TH D.L.I. BATTALION BATTLE ORDER. The Battⁿ formed up on a double company front- with "A" Coy on the RIGHT and "B" Coy on the LEFT. "C" and "D" Coy in support - on RIGHT and LEFT respectively. Each company was in 3 waves + each wave in 2 lines. The distance between waves was 20 yards + between lines 10 yards. Company HQ were in rear of their waves + Battⁿ HQRS in rear of 8TH WAVE.	

WAR DIARY or INTELLIGENCE SUMMARY

Army Form C. 2118

Place	Date	Hour	Summary of Events and Information	Remarks and references to Appendices
	7/6/17.		OBJECTIVES. I. RED LINE just S.E. of FIKHOF FARM & about 100 yds in advance of it. II. BLUE LINE ie. DAMSTRASSE. LINE OF MARCH - 155° True.	
	7/6/17	1 A.M.	Battⁿ formed up with 1st wave in our front-line.	
	"	2·55AM	The front wave advanced to within 75 yds of the enemy front-line & the rear waves conformed to this movement. At this time the night was very quiet. The enemy commenced to put up a number of GOLDEN-RAIN LIGHTS from his front-line & our night & a few minutes later did the same on our front.	
	7/6/17	3·10AM	ZERO HOUR. A large mine was blown (by us) on our Right in the ST ELOI CRATERS and our barrage opened on the enemy front line. The intensity of the barrage was extreme.	
	"	3·13AM	At Zero plus 3 minutes the barrage lifted from the enemy front line & the leading wave entered it with no opposition as it appeared to be unoccupied. The advance then continued to the enemy support line where the first wave halted for the purpose of mopping up. None was required as the trench was completely demolished & they advanced again. At this point the 5TH wave, which was employed as a carrying party, dumped its load & went forward as a fighting wave. The 2ND WAVE followed the barrage & halted at the RED LINE where a few enemy were encountered (About 8)	

WAR DIARY
or
INTELLIGENCE SUMMARY
(Erase heading not required.)

Army Form C. 2118

PAGE 3

Place	Date	Hour	Summary of Events and Information	Remarks and references to Appendices
	7/6/17	3.30 AM	It was between this line & the enemy support line that the enemy barrage fell, though it was very ragged. The 3rd, 4th & 8th waves moved straight on to the BLUE LINE, the 2nd objective (DAMSTRASSE) which they carried with considerable dash although enfiladed by M.G. fire from the direction of WHITE CHATEAU and THE STABLES. About 30 Germans were taken prisoner & an equal number killed. A line of posts was rapidly dug in front of the DAMSTRASSE.	
	7/6/17	5 AM	protected by Lewis Gun posts pushed forward. This line afforded good cover by 5 A.M. Very little resistance was encountered at all during the attack and the prisoners taken were entirely demoralised. The line must have been lightly held or evacuated since few enemy dead were seen. The 8th LONDON REGT on our left were held up for some time by M.G. fire from WHITE CHATEAU. Whilst digging in & afterwards during the day very very little hostile shell fire was experienced. It was even possible to bring up pack animals to the DAMSTRASSE while it was still light. Battalion Headquarters were established at O 9 C 88.	

Army Form C. 2118

WAR DIARY
or
INTELLIGENCE SUMMARY
(Erase heading not required.)

Place	Date	Hour	Summary of Events and Information	Remarks and references to Appendices
DAMSTRASSE	7/6/17	6:30 AM.	At zero plus 3 hours 50 minutes the 122nd Inf. Brigade attacked through our line (BLUE LINE) accompanied by Tanks & captured the BLACK LINE (OBLONG RESERVE & OBSCURE TRENCH) This caused no hostile retaliation on our position.	
"		3:10 P.M.	At zero plus 12 hours the 24TH DIVISION also attack through our line & captured a line of trenches about 150 yds in front of the BLACK LINE GROUND. The ground attacked over was very much cut up by shell fire & almost all trenches obliterated so that some difficulty was experienced in recognizing any particular portion of the enemy's lines. Early in the attack Major Wardell was seriously wounded in the head. Captain Spencer Cox then took command of the Battalion until the arrival of Captain T. Kelly. M.C who had been in reserve.	
			CASUALTIES.	
			CAPT W.J. HEDLEY KILLED.	
			LIEUT A. McKENZIE "	
			2/LT T.B. SMITH "	
			2/LT T. MARTIN "	

WAR DIARY
or
INTELLIGENCE SUMMARY

(Erase heading not required.)

Army Form C. 2118

Place	Date	Hour	Summary of Events and Information	Remarks and references to Appendices
DAMSTRASSE	7/6/17	—	CASUALTIES :— KILLED — 4 Officers and 29 other ranks. WOUNDED — 5 Officers + 157 other ranks. Officers wounded were :— MAJOR H. WARDELL. 2/LT W.H.F. COURTHOPE. 2/LT H.O. LOVE. 2/LT A.E. RYAN. 2/LT A.W. PRICE.	
	8/6/17	7.30 P.M.	During the day there was little hostile shelling until the evening directed against our trench. The woods in front of the Batt^{ns} position were heavily shelled at intervals. The enemy counter attacked but were repulsed by our barrage before reaching the front line. This Battⁿ (in support) lost no casualties. The remainder of the night was quiet.	
	9/6/17		The hostile artillery was more active & caused a few casualties. The spirit of the troops was excellent. All rations had been delivered without a hitch & the men were able to make fires & boil water. The weather continued fine. 2/LT A.F. UNDERHAY was wounded by a small fragment of shell.	

Army Form C. 2118

WAR DIARY
or
INTELLIGENCE SUMMARY

(Erase heading not required.)

Instructions regarding War Diaries and Intelligence Summaries are contained in F. S. Regs., Part II. and the Staff Manual respectively. Title Pages will be prepared in manuscript.

Place	Date	Hour	Summary of Events and Information	Remarks and references to Appendices
DAMSTRASSE	10/6/17	—	The enemy artillery was again more active & also his aeroplanes which flew low over our lines. At about 10 P.M. the enemy put up a red light which was mistaken by some of the troops in the front line for our S.O.S. signal. As a result others were put up & the enemy artillery & our own opened with barrage fire. This gradually subsided & at about 11.30 P.M. all was quiet & remained so throughout the night.	
	10/6/17	10 P.M.		
	11/6/17	—	Nothing of importance occurred.	
	12/6/17	6.13 P.M.	The enemy artillery was fairly quiet. At 6.13 P.M. the Battⁿ was relieved by the 15TH HAMPSHIRE REGT less 2 Companies. The Battⁿ proceeded to VOORMEZEELE where they occupied bivouacs in the vicinity of MAGGEE TRENCH and MIDDLESEX LANE. The relief was carried out without casualties & was complete by 8.30 P.M. 2/Lt D.C.H. O'Byrne returned to duty with the Battⁿ from 33rd "Prisoners of War" Company.	
VOORMEZEELE	13/4/17		The 13TH JUNE was spent in resting & cleaning up.	
	14/6/17		Companies reorganized their bombers, Lewis Gun teams, etc. A working party of 1 Offr & 70 ORs went out to bury cable.	

WAR DIARY or INTELLIGENCE SUMMARY

Army Form C. 2118

(Erase heading not required.)

Instructions regarding War Diaries and Intelligence Summaries are contained in F.S. Regs., Part II. and the Staff Manual respectively. Title Pages will be prepared in manuscript.

Place	Date	Hour	Summary of Events and Information	Remarks and references to Appendices
NEUVE EGLISE.	15/6/17	—	Rest in Vormezeele continued.	
	16/6/17	—	"	2/Lt D.C.H. O'Byrne was wounded whilst on a working party.
	17/6/17	—	"	
	18/6/17	—	"	
OLD FRENCH TRENCH	19/6/17	At 2.30 P.M. moved into BRIGADE RESERVE in OLD FRENCH TRENCH. The move was completed by 5 P.M.	
	20/6/17		The Battn. remained in OLD FRENCH TRENCH and found working parties of about 200 men each night for working on forward communication tunnels.	
	21/6/17		On 21st June - Lt Col R. Otter M.C. returned & resumed command of the Battn.	
	22/6/17			
	23/6/17			
	24/6/17	8 P.M.	The Battn. relieved the 23RD MIDDLESEX REGT in the RIGHT SUB-SECTOR of the Brigade. DISPOSITION. FRONT LINE - "D" COY. SUPPORT LINE - "B" & "C" COYS RESERVE LINE - "A" COY The relief was carried out without casualties & was complete by 12.30 A.M. 25/6/17. BN HQRS at O 3 d 8.7.	

WAR DIARY or INTELLIGENCE SUMMARY

Army Form C. 2118

Place	Date	Hour	Summary of Events and Information	Remarks and references to Appendices
	25/8/17		The front & support lines (GREEN & BLACK) were shelled intermittently & also the surrounding woods. "B" Coy relieved "D" Coy in front line	
	26/8/17		Intermittent shelling as yesterday. The trenches were very muddy & in places about 6 inches deep in water. Enemy aircraft active & fired MGs into GREEN & BLUE lines. Many planes had red fuselages.	
		5:30 PM	A shell of large calibre (5.9) burst in the dugout occupied by CAPT T. KELLY and killed CAPT. T. KELLY M.C. 2/Lt W.A.L. ROBINSON. 2/Lt H.N.F. COOK.	
	27/8/17		"C" Coy relieved "D" Coy in front line. The day was quiet except for the usual shelling of woods & GREEN & BLACK LINES. The following awards were made for distinguished action in the field on 7/8/17.	
			No G.11160 Pte E. Sale. Howlett. H.F. " G.10591 " Cook. J.C. " G.11564 " Finlayson. R.A. MILITARY MEDALS " G.11290 " Douglas. P.W. " G.10934 L/Cpl Caple C.T. " G.11246 " Dod. A.W. " G.6646 "	

WAR DIARY
or
INTELLIGENCE SUMMARY
(Erase heading not required.)

Army Form C. 2118

Place	Date	Hour	Summary of Events and Information	Remarks and references to Appendices
	27/6/17.	10 P.M.	The Batt'n was relieved by the 23RD MIDDLESEX REGT & proceeded to CONVENT LANE less "D" C'y which moved into D TUNNEL on left of CANAL at SPOILBANK at LOCK 7. Relief was complete by 12 MIDNIGHT.	
	28/6/17.	—	Batt'n remained in CONVENT LANE	
	29/6/17.			
	30/6/17.		At 8.30 P.M. the Batt'n proceeded to ALBERTA CAMP for the night. No unit took over position held.	
			CASUALTIES - from JUNE 8TH to JUNE 30TH.	
			OFFICERS - 3 KILLED - 1 WOUNDED.	
			O.Rs - 10 " 29 "	

R. Otter Lt Col
O.C. 11 Queens

SECRET.   APPENDIX I   Copy No...13....
                                  Wardell

OPERATION ORDER No. 9.
By.
Major H. WARDELL.
Commanding 11th. (S) Battn. "THE QUEEN'S" (R.W.S) Regiment.
----

1. **INTENTION.** The Second Army will be ready to make an attack at any time after 31st. MAY, 1917.
   The 123rd. Brigade will attack on the LEFT of the 41st. Divisional Front.
   The 124th. Brigade being on the RIGHT.
   The 8th Battalion LONDON Regiment of the 142nd. Brigade (47th. Division) will be on the LEFT.

2. **DISPOSITION of BRIGADE.** The line to be taken by the 123rd. Brigade is from O. 3.c.15.75. to O. 3.b.4.9. and the disposition will be as follows:-

   On the RIGHT, 23rd. MIDDLESEX Regiment.
   In the CENTRE, 10th. ROYAL WEST KENT Regiment.
   On the LEFT, 11th. QUEEN'S Regiment.
   In SUPPORT, 20th. DURHAM LIGHT INFANTRY.

3. **BATTALION BATTLE ORDER.** The 11th. QUEEN'S will attack on a double Company front (frontage about 220 yards).
   "A" Company on the RIGHT.
   "B"   "   "   " LEFT.
   "C" and "D" Companies in SUPPORT on RIGHT and LEFT respectively.
   Each Company will be in three waves, each wave being in two lines.
   Distance between waves 20 yards, with 10 yards between lines.
   Company Head-Quarters will advance in rear of their last wave.
   Battalion Head-Quarters in rear of last wave of the Battalion.

4. **DAYS PRIOR TO ATTACK.** The attack will take place on ZERO day, which will be known as "Z" day. Preceding 5 days are referred to as "Y", "X", "W", "V", and "U" days.
   The days after "Z" day as "A", "B", and "C".

5. **OBJECTIVES.** There are two Objectives for the Battalion.
   (1) RED Line just S.E. Of EIKHOF FARM and about 100 yards in advance of it. The Line is imaginary and will be marked by our Barrage.
   (2) BLUE Line, i.e. THE DAMSTRASSE.
   There is a 3rd Objective known as the BLACK Line which will be taken by the 122nd. Brigade which will pass through the 123rd. Brigade.
   The 122nd. Brigade will form up in rear of the DAMSTRASSE at ZERO + 3 hours. By ZERO plus 3.40, they will form up under our Standing Barrage and go forward to the attack on the BLACK Line consisting of Obstacle Switch, OBSCURE TRENCH, OBLONG RESERVE.
   At ZERO plus 10 hours, the attack will be continued by the 24th. Division.

6. **BARRAGE.** (Time Table). At ZERO plus 3 Barrage will lift off Enemy FRONT LINE
   "   "   " 8   "   "   "   "   "   "   SUPPORT LINE.
   "   "   " 20   "   "   "   "   "   " Front of RED LINE
   "   "   " 35   "   "   "   "   "   "   The DAMSTRASSE.
   "   "   " 45   "   "   "   "   "   "

7. **DISPOSITIONS.** (Previous to attack). The Battalion will enter the Line on W/X and X/Y nights and will attack at ZERO hour on "Z" day. Dispositions as per instructions issued.

8. **BOUNDARIES.** The Battalion RIGHT Boundary is the Tramline running N. and S. just E. of EIKHOF FARM.
   LEFT Boundary is the Road S. of OAR ALLEY.
   Line of March 155° (true).

9.	**ASSEMBLY & ASSAULT.**	The Battalion will be formed up with the First Wave in our Front Line two hours before ZERO.
Communication must be established on both flanks.
The First Wave will move from our Front Line to 75 yards from enemy Front Line, close under the Barrage, to be in position by ZERO - rear Waves will conform.
Tapes will be put out from Front Line to show the direction. Should they fail <u>COMPASS BEARING MUST BE STRICTLY FOLLOWED.</u>
At ZERO plus 3, the Artillery will lift from the enemy Front Line and the leading Wave having crept as near as possible to enemy line, will push in followed by the other Waves.
10.	**MOPPERS.**	Officers Commanding Companies will nominate necessary men up to 50% of their strength to mop up as required.
These men to wear a white band on left arm and their special tasks will be allotted to them. Half a Platoon of the 20th DURHAM LIGHT INFANTRY will follow and assist the first Wave, and half a Platoon the second Wave.
The Mopping Party of DURHAM LIGHT INFANTRY attached to the second Wave, will mop up and thoroughly clear enemy Front Line.
11.	**PROGRESS of WAVES.**	The First Wave will halt in enemy Support Line with its party of moppers of the DURHAM LIGHT INFANTRY.
Having thoroughly mopped up this line, it will hand same over to the 7th. Wave (DURHAM LIGHT INFANTRY) and move straight forward to strengthen the 6th. Wave on the Outpost Line in FRONT of the DAMSTRASSE.
The Second Wave will follow the Barrage, halting at the RED Line until it reaches the new enemy Reserve Trench (between RED Line and the DAMSTRASSE) and mop same and remain there in reserve at the call of the troops in the DAMSTRASSE.
The 3rd., 4th., and 6th., Waves move straight on to the Assault on the 2nd. Objective - the DAMSTRASSE itself.
The 5th. Wave acts as carrying party to the Battalion and on arrival in enemy Support Line, will dump its load consisting of Wire, Sandbags, Bombs, Grenades, S.A.A. etc and will then go forward as a fighting Wave without loss of time. (The material so dumped, will be collected as soon as possible by the DURHAM LIGHT INFANTRY, who will carry it forward to the DAMSTRASSE when called for by the advanced troops). The 5th. Wave will then join the 3rd., 4th., and 6th. Waves in their Assault on the DAMSTRASSE, as above.
As early as possible, the 6th. Wave will push forward beyond the DAMSTRASSE where they will form a line of Outposts close up to the Standing Barrage.
The 1st Wave should by this time, be up to assist in this work and will also be re-inforced by troops from the DAMSTRASSE as circumstances permit.
Moppers will work where necessary and special parties previously detailed, will deal with enemy strong points.
7th and 8th. Waves xxxxxxxx composed of the DURHAM LIGHT INFANTRY will halt in enemy Front and Support LINE mop and dig in.
12.	**BATTALION RESERVE.**	Officers Commanding Companies will each detail their spare Lewis Gun Section to Battalion Head-Quarters, with which they will march under direct orders of the Commanding Officer.
13.	**VICKERS GUNS.**	Three are allotted to the Battalion. They will follow as an extra Wave immediately behind the 6th. Wave and move forward to the Outpost Line and to be established there.
14.	**STOKES GUNS.**	One is allotted to the Battalion, and will move in rear of Battalion Head-Quarters and will act as directed by the Commanding Officer.
15.	**ENEMY DUG-OUTS.**	These will be mopped up by respective Mopping Parties as detailed to Company Commanders. They will work down trenches from the flanks until they meet each other - thus ensuring no Dug-Outs are missed.

16. **STRONG POINT.**   Strong Point will be established under the direction of Officer Commanding "D" Company at O.5.c.6.7.

17. **INTER-COMMUNI-CATION.**   Great care must be taken to keep in touch with the troops on either flank and all Officers must be prepared to assist adjoining Units in case of necessity.
    In the event of troops failing to obtain their objective, a defensive flank must be formed by the leading troops. Officers commanding "A" and "C" will be prepared to assist the 10th ROYAL WEST KENT Regiment should they be held up at EIKHOF FARM.

18. **FLARES.**   Flares will be carried by all Sections, but only the foremost wave must light them. Great care must be taken that no other troops are in front.

19. **RE-ORGANISATION & CONSOLIDATION**   All ranks must be made to realise that when the Objective is reached, consolidation and re-organisation against counter-attacks, is absolutely essential and must be carried out before the troops can rest.

20. **EQUIPMENT etc.**   As detailed in Appendix A.

21. **RATIONS & WATER.**   As detailed in Appendix B.

22. **REGIMENTAL AID POSTS.**   The Regimental Aid Post is situated in OLD FRENCH TRENCH.
    Prisoners may be utilised for carrying wounded.

23. **PRISONERS.**   Prisoners will be marched back under Company arrangements to Brigade Cage at Junction of CONVENT LANE and VOORMEZEELE - YPRES ROAD. They will be marshalled in groups of not less than ten if possible, with an escort of 10%.

24. **REPORTS.**   Officers Commanding Companies will report to Battalion Head-Quarters on completion of Assembly and render Situation and Progress Reports every half hour.
    Special Reports will be rendered as necessary, bearing in mind that Negative Reports or information are as valuable as Positive.
    When the Battalion has advanced, Head-Quarters will be between enemy Support and Red Line until DAMSTRASSE is made good.
    Casualty reports must be returned if and when 10% casualties have been sustained.

Duplicates

SECRET.   Copy No. 16

OPERATION ORDER No. 9.
By.
Major H. WARDELL.
Commanding 11th. (S) Battn. "THE QUEEN'S" (R.W.S) Regiment.

---

1. **INTENTION.** The Second Army will be ready to make an attack at any time after 31st. MAY, 1917.
    The 123rd. Brigade will attack on the LEFT of the 41st. Divisional Front.
    The 124th. Brigade being on the RIGHT.
    The 8th Battalion LONDON Regiment of the 142nd. Brigade (47th. Division) will be on the LEFT.

2. **DISPOSITION of BRIGADE.** The line to be taken by the 123rd. Brigade is from O. 3. c. 15. 75. to O. 3. b. 4. 9. and the disposition will be as follows:-

    On the RIGHT, 23rd. MIDDLESEX Regiment.
    In the CENTRE, 10th. ROYAL WEST KENT Regiment.
    On the LEFT, 11th. QUEEN'S Regiment.
    In SUPPORT, 20th. DURHAM LIGHT INFANTRY.

3. **BATTALION BATTLE ORDER.** The 11th. QUEEN'S will attack on a double Company front (frontage about 320 yards).
    "A" Company on the RIGHT.
    "B"   "   "   " LEFT.
    "C" and "D" Companies in SUPPORT on RIGHT and LEFT respectively.
    Each Company will be in three waves, each wave being in two lines.
    Distance between waves 20 yards, with 10 yards between lines.
    Company Head-Quarters will advance in rear of their last wave.
    Battalion Head-Quarters in rear of last wave of the Battalion.

4. **DAYS PRIOR TO ATTACK.** The attack will take place on ZERO day, which will be known as "Z" day. Preceding 5 days are referred to as "Y", "X", "W", "V", and "U" days.
    The days after "Z" day as "A", "B", and "C".

5. **OBJECTIVES.** There are two Objectives for the Battalion.
    (1) RED Line just S.E. Of EIKHOF FARM and about 100 yards in advance of it. The Line is imaginary and will be marked by our Barrage.
    (2) BLUE Line, i.e. THE DAMSTRASSE.
    There is a 3rd Objective known as the BLACK Line which will be taken by the 122nd. Brigade which will pass through the 123rd. Brigade.
    The 122nd. Brigade will form up in rear of the DAMSTRASSE at ZERO + 3 hours. By ZERO plus 3.40, they will form up under our Standing Barrage and go forward to the attack on the BLACK Line consisting of Obstacle Switch, OBSCURE TRENCH, OBLONG RESERVE.
    At ZERO plus 10 hours, the attack will be continued by the 24th. Division.

6. **BARRAGE.** (Time Table).
    At ZERO plus 3   Barrage will be off Enemy FRONT LINE
    "   "   " 20   "   "   "   "   "   SUPPORT LINE
    "   "   " 35   "   "   "   "   "   Front of RED LINE
    "   "   " 45   "   "   "   "   "   The DAMSTRASSE.

7. **DISPOSITIONS.** (Previous to attack). The Battalion will enter the Line on W/X and X/Y nights and will attack at ZERO hour on "Z" day. Dispositions as per instructions issued.

8. **BOUNDARIES.** The Battalion RIGHT Boundary is the Tramline running N. and S. just E. of EIKHOF FARM.
    LEFT Boundary is the Road S. of OAR ALLEY.
    Line of March 155° (true).

9.	ASSEMBLY & ASSAULT.	The Battalion will be formed up with the First Wave in our Front Line two hours before ZERO.
Communication must be established on both flanks.
The First Wave will move from our Front Line to 75 yards from enemy Front Line, close under the Barrage, to be in position by ZERO – rear Waves will conform.
Tapes will be put out from Front Line to show the direction. Should they fail COMPASS BEARING MUST BE STRICTLY FOLLOWED.
At ZERO plus 3, the Artillery will lift from the enemy Front Line and the leading Wave having crept as near as possible to enemy line, will push in followed by the other Waves.
10.	MOPPERS.	Officers Commanding Companies will nominate necessary men up to 50% of their strength to mop up as required.
These men to wear a white band on left arm and their special tasks will be allotted to them. Half a Platoon of the 20th DURHAM LIGHT INFANTRY will follow and assist the first Wave, and half a Platoon the second Wave.
The Mopping Party of DURHAM LIGHT INFANTRY attached to the second Wave, will mop up and thoroughly clear enemy Front Line.
11.	PROGRESS of WAVES.	The First Wave will halt in enemy Support Line with its party of moppers of the DURHAM LIGHT INFANTRY.
Having thoroughly mopped up this line, it will hand same over to the 7th. Wave (DURHAM LIGHT INFANTRY) and move straight forward to strengthen the 6th. Wave on the Outpost Line in FRONT of the DAMSTRASSE.
The Second Wave will follow the Barrage, halting at the RED Line until it reaches the new enemy Reserve Trench (between RED Line and the DAMSTRASSE) and mop same and remain there in reserve at the call of the troops in the DAMSTRASSE.
The 3rd., 4th., and 6th., Waves move straight on to the Assault on the 2nd. Objective – the DAMSTRASSE itself.
The 5th. Wave acts as carrying party to the Battalion and on arrival in enemy Support Line, will dump its load consisting of Wire, Sandbags, Bombs, Grenades, S.A.A. etc and will then go forward as a fighting Wave without loss of time. (The material so dumped, will be collected as soon as possible by the DURHAM LIGHT INFANTRY, who will carry it forward to the DAMSTRASSE when called for by the advanced troops). The 5th. Wave will then join the 3rd., 4th., and 6th. Waves in their Assault on the DAMSTRASSE, as above.
As early as possible, the 6th. Wave will push forward beyond the DAMSTRASSE where they will form a line of Outposts close up to the Standing Barrage.
The 1st Wave should by this time, be up to assist in this work and will also be re-inforced by troops from the DAMSTRASSE as circumstances permit.
Moppers will work where necessary and special parties previously detailed, will deal with enemy strong points.
7th and 8th. Waves composed of the DURHAM LIGHT INFANTRY will halt in enemy Front and Support LINES mop and dig in.
12.	BATTALION RESERVE.	Officers Commanding Companies will each detail their spare Lewis Gun Section to Battalion Head-Quarters, with which they will march under direct orders of the Commanding Officer.
13.	VICKERS GUNS.	Three are allotted to the Battalion. They will follow as an extra Wave immediately behind the 6th. Wave and move forward to the Outpost Line and to be established there.
14.	STOKES GUNS.	One is allotted to the Battalion, and will move in rear of Battalion Head-Quarters and will act as directed by the Commanding Officer.
15.	ENEMY DUG-OUTS.	These will be mopped up by respective Mopping Parties as detailed to Company Commanders. They will work down trenches from the flanks until they meet each other – thus ensuring no Dug-Outs are missed.

16.	STRONG POINT.	Strong Point will be established under the direction of Officer Commanding "D" Company at O. 3.d.8.7.
17.	INTER-COMMUNI- CATION.	Great care must be taken to keep in touch with the troops on either flank and all Officers must be prepared to assist adjoining Units in case of necessity.

In the event of troops failing to obtain their objective, a defensive flank must be formed by the leading troops. Officers commanding "A" and "C" will be prepared to assist the 10th ROYAL WEST KENT Regiment should they be held up at EIKHOF FARM.

18.	FLARES.	Flares will be carried by all Sections, but only the foremost Wave must light them. Great care must be taken that no other troops are in front.
19.	RE-ORGANISATION & CONSOLIDATION	All ranks must be made to realise that when the objective is reached, consolidation and re-organisation against counter-attacks, is absolutely essential and must be carried out before the troops can rest.
20.	EQUIPMENT etc.	As detailed in Appendix A.
21.	RATIONS & WATER.	As detailed in Appendix B.
22.	REGIMENTAL AID POSTS.	The Regimental Aid Post is situated in OLD FRENCH TRENCH.

Prisoners may be utilised for carrying wounded.

23.	PRISONERS.	Prisoners will be marched back under Company arrangements to Brigade Cage at junction of CONVENT LANE and VOORMEZEELE - YPRES ROAD. They will be marshalled in groups of not less than ten if possible, with an escort of 10%.
24.	REPORTS.	Officers Commanding Companies will report to Battalion Head-Quarters on completion of Assembly and render Situation and Progress Reports every half hour.

Special Reports will be rendered as necessary, bearing in mind that Negative Reports or information are as valuable as Positive.

When the Battalion has advanced, Head-Quarters will be between enemy Support and Red Line until DAMSTRASSE is made good.

Casualty reports must be returned if and when 40% casualties have been sustained.

War Diary

ADDITIONS AND ALTERATIONS TO OPERATION ORDER No. 9.

Amendment to Barrage Time Table paragraph 6.

At + 3	Barrage lifts off	FRONT LINE.
At 8	" " "	SUPPORT.
At 12	" " "	Imaginary Line 100^X S. of SUPPORT.
At 20	" " "	RED Line.
At 35	" " "	New Support in Front of DAMSTRASSE.
At 39	" " "	Trench immediately in Front of DAMSTRASSE
At 45	" " "	DAMSTRASSE (East only).
At 49	" " "	Imaginary Line 200^X S. of DAMSTRASSE (on the EAST) and WEST End of DAMSTRASSE.

Officers Commanding Companies will ensure that all their men are equipped with Ammunition, Bombs, Tools, etc., in accordance with Appendix "A". These will be drawn from Dumps on "Y" Day.

- from -

"A" Company and 1 Platoon "B" Company/Dump in OLD FRENCH TRENCH.

"B" Company (2 Platoons)) from Dump Near Junction of
"C"   "   ) CONVENT LANE & VOORMEZEELE
                                                              SWITCH

"D"   "   from Dump G.H.Q. Advanced Line.

For the fifth (carrying) Waves, "C" and "D" Companies will draw material, S.A.A., etc., from their respective Dumps as above. Each half of this Wave will carry,

10 Coils Barbed Wire.
500 Sandbags.
10 Boxes Bombs (Mills No. 5).

At 12.30 AM night 6/7 June Bn marched out to tapes laid out behind our front line between O 3 c 13.75 + O 3 b 4 2 . The Right flank being on the rt-ft the 19UD PATCH & the left on the left of TRIANGULAR WOOD. On the Right were the 10th R W K Regt & on the left the 8TH LONDON REGT (47th DIV) In support 20 DLI.

BATTN BATTLE ORDER. The Batt'n formed up as a double Coy front with A Coy on the Rt & "B" Coy on left + "C" + "D" in support on Rt & Lt respectively.

Each company was in 3 waves + each wave in 2 lines. The distances between waves was 30 yds + between lines 10 yds.

Company H.Q. advanced in rear of their last wave — B Coy HQ in rear of 1st Wave.

OBJECTIVES. I Known as RED LINE JuN.S.E.1/F1K40 FM Run. of Orkus.

LINE OF MARCH is 158° True.

1 AM. Batt formed up with yds Wave in our front line. 2 hrs before Zero.

2.53 AM. First wave advanced to within 75 yds of enemy front line & 2nd wave conformed to this movement. At this time the night was very quiet — a few field guns only were in action some distance to our R.I. The enemy continued to put up a number of GOLDEN RAIN FLARES from his front line on our Right & later did the same on our front.

ZERO — On our Right a large mine was blown in S.27.O.1 CRATERS Barrage opened

3.10 a.m.

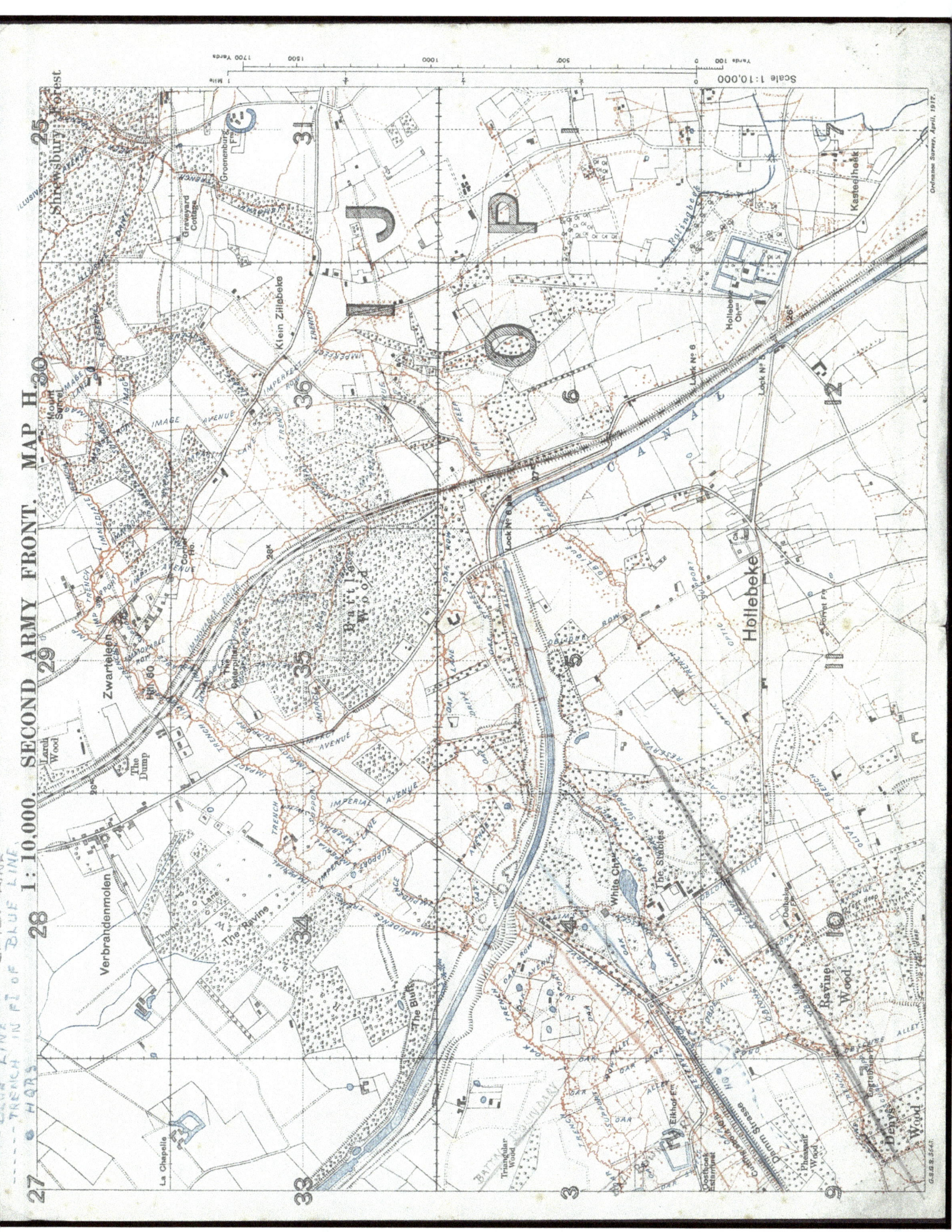

APPENDIX II

Army Form C. 2118.

XI RW Surrey 123/21

Vol 15

16

WAR DIARY
or
INTELLIGENCE SUMMARY
(Erase heading not required.)

Place	Date	Hour	Summary of Events and Information	Remarks and references to Appendices
MONT de CATS	1/11/17		Battalion in billets. The usual training took place daily	
"	7/11/17		Major A Hardell was awarded the D.S.O. for gallantry on the 7th of June. C/4716 Pte J Morley was awarded a Bar to the Military Medal for gallantry on the 7th of June.	
WESTOUTRE	22/11/17 23/11/17		Bn moved to WESTOUTRE and bivouaced there until the 24th. C.O. and all O.C. Coys went up to the line to view the ground on which the Bn were expected to form up at a later date.	
DE-ZON	24/11/17		The Bn moved to DE-ZON Camp for 24 hours.	
IMPERIAL TRENCH	25/11/17		Bn started for the trenches at 3pm to relieve the 23rd Bn The London Regt. This relief took practically all night owing to the bad state of the ground and the heavy shelling.	

Army Form C. 2118.

WAR DIARY
or
INTELLIGENCE SUMMARY
(Erase heading not required.)

Instructions regarding War Diaries and Intelligence Summaries are contained in F. S. Regs., Part II. and the Staff Manual respectively. Title Pages will be prepared in manuscript.

Place	Date	Hour	Summary of Events and Information	Remarks and references to Appendices
IMPERIAL TRENCH	25/7/17		These trenches consisted of groups of outposts. A, B Coys in advance C Coy in Support and D Coy in Reserve. The Reserve Coy were quartered in the original British front line. RAT LANE & DEANSGATE.	
	26/7/17		Shelling was fairly heavy during the day. A 5.9 shell dropped on a party of B Coy killing 6 and wounding 8. The total casualties for the day were 9 killed & 14 wounded	
	27/7/17		Nothing of any importance happened in the line. The Bn Transport were heavily shelled whilst bringing up rations during the afternoon, 1 man being killed and 2 wounded Capt W.L.S. Cox who was with this party was also wounded.	

Army Form C. 2118.

WAR DIARY
or
INTELLIGENCE SUMMARY
(Erase heading not required.)

Instructions regarding War Diaries and Intelligence Summaries are contained in F. S. Regs., Part II. and the Staff Manual respectively. Title Pages will be prepared in manuscript.

Place	Date	Hour	Summary of Events and Information	Remarks and references to Appendices
IMPERIAL TRENCH	28/11/17		In the early hours tapes were laid out by Lieut Darlington to mark the forming up spot for the Bn in the impending attack. This duty was not altogether finished owing to Machine gun and rifle fire.	
"	29/11/17		The tapes were finished and all Officers & NCOs has been over the ground either on the 28th or 29th.	
"	30/11/17		The day has passed quietly. During the evening 2 Pioneers cut steps in the Railway Embankment over which the Bn had to cross to reach the forming up tapes later in the night. These steps were invaluable as the ground was of a very greasy nature.	

Army Form C. 2118.

WAR DIARY
or
INTELLIGENCE SUMMARY
(Erase heading not required.)

Instructions regarding War Diaries and Intelligence Summaries are contained in F. S. Regs., Part II. and the Staff Manual respectively. Title Pages will be prepared in manuscript.

Place	Date	Hour	Summary of Events and Information	Remarks and references to Appendices
IMPERIAL TRENCH.	3/1/17		The Bn moved off at 9-40 pm to line up on the tape	
	31/1/17		The Bn were in position about 1-30 am without suffering a casualty of any description and without the slightest hitch. ZERO hour was at 3.50 am. The Bn moved forward with the Barrage and experienced no difficulty in taking the first objective. It was found that, owing to the heavy state of the ground, the troops had great difficulty in keeping up to the Barrage which was gradually creeping away. At about 300 yds from the final objective 3 concrete shelters were found; these shelters were held by the enemy with machine guns and apparently picked rifle men.	

Army Form C. 2118.

WAR DIARY
or
INTELLIGENCE SUMMARY
(Erase heading not required.)

Instructions regarding War Diaries and Intelligence Summaries are contained in F. S. Regs., Part II. and the Staff Manual respectively. Title Pages will be prepared in manuscript.

Place	Date	Hour	Summary of Events and Information	Remarks and references to Appendices
BATTLE FIELD	3/4/17		The Barrage on the previous bombardment had made no impression on these "pots", and the tapping of them by infantry bombers on the impossible. A party of 50 men under 2/Lt Ryan, and another party of 53 under 2/Lt Ford. Martin got to within 50" of these shelters. These parties suffered heavily as it was almost impossible to stir without an enemy machine gun firing. During the night these parties withdrew, and joined the remainder of the Bn at the 2nd Objective. Capt Borden with C Coy had also been held up by these same concrete shelters and had linked up with the R W KENTS also at the 2nd Objective	

Army Form C. 2118.

WAR DIARY
or
INTELLIGENCE SUMMARY

(Erase heading not required.)

Instructions regarding War Diaries and Intelligence Summaries are contained in F. S. Regs., Part II. and the Staff Manual respectively. Title Pages will be prepared in manuscript.

Place	Date	Hour	Summary of Events and Information	Remarks and references to Appendices
BATTLE FIELD	31/7/1		The casualties on this day were Lieut A.J. SMITH killed, Lieut KITCHINGMAN wounded, Lieut E. APTED Missing. O Ranks casualties were estimated at 200.	

R. Otter.
Lt. Colonel.
Commanding 11th Bn. "The Queen's" Regt.

OPERATION ORDER
- by -
Lieut. Colonel R. OTTER M.C.
Commanding 11th. (S) Battn. "THE QUEEN'S" (R.W.S) Regt.

No. 10.
18th. July, 1917.

DUTIES of WAVES.

2nd. WAVE. :- Mops RED LINE, carries and dumps in same line. They will consolidate and make strong points in front of RED LINE. A special strong point being made by "B" Company at corner of wood, O.6.a.9.7.

1st. WAVE. :- Mops BLUE LINE. They will consolidate in front of BLUE LINE. Special strong points at O.6.d.25.80. by "A" Company and at O.6.b.50.50. by "B" Company.

3rd. WAVE. :- Mops and consolidates GREEN LINE.

4th. WAVE. :- Carries as far as BLUE LINE, then go on past GREEN LINE and form outpost line under the barrage. Consolidate shell holes.

5th. WAVE. :- Concentrate on Battalion Head-Quarters.

(Sgd) G. PANNALL
2/Lieut.
Acting Adjutant.

11th. (S) Battn. "THE QUEEN'S" (R.W.S) Regt.

OPERATION ORDER
- by -
Lieut. Colonel R. OTTER M.C.
Commanding 11th. (S) Battn. "THE QUEEN'S" (R.W.S) Regt.

No. 11.
18th. July, 1917.

TIME TABLE.

ZERO.:- Barrage falls on RED LINE.   Battalion moves forward as near Barrage as possible, about 75 yards from German Line.

ZERO + 4.   Barrage lifts.   Battalion assaults RED LINE.

ZERO + 28.   Barrage lifts off BLUE LINE.   Battalion assault this Line.

ZERO + 40.   Barrage dwells on GREEN LINE sufficiently long to indicate position of this Line.

ZERO + 45   Barrage lifts off GREEN LINE and creeps on about 4 400 yards followed by the 4th. Wave, who will consolidate shell holes when the Barrage finally halts.

(Sgd). C. PANNALL
2/Lieut.
Acting Adjutant
11th. (S) Battn. "THE QUEEN'S" (R.W.S) Regt.

WAR DIARY or INTELLIGENCE SUMMARY

11 RW Surrey Regt

Army Form C. 2118.

Place	Date	Hour	Summary of Events and Information	Remarks and references to Appendices
	1917 Aug 1st		The Battalion continued to hold the line until the night of the 1st/2nd August when they were relieved by the 10th Battn The Queens. The relief was carried out with great difficulty as the conditions were extremely bad, owing to the amount of rain that had fallen during the preceding 48 hours.	
	2nd		2nd Lieut. A.E. RYAN M.C. and 2nd Lieut. A.P.D. LODGE were reported wounded together with 40 other Ranks. Lieut E. APTED and 41 other Ranks reported missing. The Battalion, after relief, moved back to the old British front line; the Companies occupying the trenches at DEANSGATE and in the vicinity.	
	3rd		The Battalion moved to RIDGE WOOD Area and rested in tents and bivouacs.	
	5th		Details moved to ROSENHILL CAMP	
	6th		Major R.C. Smith to 20th Bn Durham Light Infantry as Commanding Officer.	
	7th		The Battalion moved to the Line, 2 Companies staying at	DEANSGATE

WAR DIARY
or
INTELLIGENCE SUMMARY

(Erase heading not required.)

Army Form C. 2118.

Place	Date	Hour	Summary of Events and Information	Remarks and references to Appendices
	1917 Aug 7th		DEANSGATE. 1 Company BATTLE WOOD and 1 Company CATERPILLAR.	
	9th		2nd Lieut N.S. FORD wounded.	
	11th		The Battalion were relieved and moved back to RIDGE WOOD Area and were quartered in tents.	
	12th	A.M. 10.45	The Battalion moved from Camp and travelled by busses to METEREN where tents had been pitched by the Advance party. The Details from ROSENHILL CAMP joined the Battalion at HALLEBAST CORNER.	(MAP REFCE X 16 a 9.6)
	13th to 17th	inclusive	Still at METEREN, the usual daily training being carried out.	
	18th	A.M. 8.15	Parade for inspection by Corps Commander.	
			Immediate awards.	
			No G.1059 Pte. H. HOWLETT Bar to Military Medal 31.7.17	
			" G.11086 Sgt. E. QUAIFE Military Medal 31.7.17 – 2.8.17	C.R.O. 1450 16.8.17
			G.10898 L/Sgt L.G. HENLEY " 31.7.17	
			G.6975 Pte. H. WRIGHT " 31.7.17	
			G.10917 " H. TOURLE " 31.7.17	
			G.11677 " F. LIGHTNING " 31.7.17	
			G.40031 " A. DIXON " 31.7.17	
			32 Other Ranks returned from Hospital, etc.	

WAR DIARY
INTELLIGENCE SUMMARY
(Erase heading not required.)

Army Form C. 2118.

Place	Date	Hour	Summary of Events and Information	Remarks and references to Appendices
	1917 Aug 19		At METEREN (X. 16 d 9.6.)	
	20	A.M. 6.30	The Battalion marched to STAPLE and arrived at 12.45 P.M. All Companies were billeted in the surrounding farms and moved next day.	
	21	A.M. 9.30	The Battalion marched from STAPLE to WIZERNES and arrived at 2.30 p.m. The whole of the Battalion, less 'B' Company was billeted in a large farm (STOCKLAND FARM) whilst 'B' Company occupied billets about 200 yards away.	
	22nd		The day was spent in cleaning billets, etc. Immediate awards. No. G 9759 L/Cpl J.E. SPRINGATE Military Medal 28.7.17 } C.R.O. G 12860 Pte J. HEMMAWAY " " 31.7.17-1.8.17 } 1461 G 11326 " C. LONGHURST " " 31.7.17 } 18-8-17.	
	23rd		Company Training.	
	24th	A.M. 11.00	Inspection of Division by F.M. Sir DOUGLAS HAIG.	
	25th		The Rifle Range was used by the Battalion, in Companies completing 3 Practices.	

WAR DIARY
INTELLIGENCE SUMMARY
(Erase heading not required.)

Army Form C. 2118.

Place	Date	Hour	Summary of Events and Information	Remarks and references to Appendices
	1917 Aug 26 to 3/9		Moral Training Immediate Awards 2nd Lieut. N.S. FORD Military Cross 31-7-17 " R.A.E. MARTIN -do- -do- 31.7.17. No G10802 C.S.M. W. QUIMBY Distinguished Conduct Medal 31-7-17 ⎫ " G11299 L/Cpl. M. HUMPHREY -do- -do- 31-7-17 ⎬ C.R.O 1509 " G10849 Sergt(A/CSM) C.K. WOODHEAD Military Medal 31.7.17 ⎭ 28.8.17 Pannall Capt a/Adjt for Lieut-Colonel Commanding 11th(S) Bn "The Queen's" (R.W.S) Regt. 13th September 1917.	

Army Form C. 2118.

WAR DIARY
or
INTELLIGENCE SUMMARY
(Erase heading not required.)

11th Queens Rl Surrey Regt
for September 1917.

Place	Date	Hour	Summary of Events and Information	Remarks and references to Appendices
Anthe at WIMEREUX			September 1917	
	1st		T 3c 66	
	2nd		Church Parade	
	3rd		Divisional Cross Country Run Teams of 20 each	
			Training Area : Platoons in the attack (all day)	
	4th		8.30 AM to 1.30 PM	
			"	
			Regimental Sports till 4 PM Officers & Ranks took great interest in	
			all the events	
	5th		Brigade Operations Horses for Coy at Training Area all day	
			Remainder of Battn on Miniature Range	
	6th		One hours parade in the morning - March to Bde Sports	
			The Battn were well represented in all events and scoring	
			good places	
	7th		Battn on Training Ground all day	
	8th		Battn went to 10.15 Miniature Range.	
			In the Afternoon marched to Divisional Race Meeting	

WAR DIARY
or
INTELLIGENCE SUMMARY

(Erase heading not required.)

Army Form C. 2118.

11 Queen Own Royal Regt.
for September 1917

Place	Date	Hour	Summary of Events and Information	Remarks and references to Appendices
	8th		Read our Ord. Sea Tent + supplies ea for the Bnde	
	9th		The Commander in Chief was present	
			Church Parade Reinforcements arrived 1 Officer 22 ORanks	
	10th		Training ava all day Attack carried out as in action	
			with an enemy	
	11th		Most of the ground was to attack viewed by all ranks	
			A good idea of the nature + defence so obtained	
			Marched to ranges 924 ×25 – Reinforcements arrived 1 Off 20 Ranks	
	12th		2/L Betts attached to Bnde as Intelligence Officer	
			Inspection of Rifles fixing Bayts &c	
			March to N22a+2 for Gas Demonstration by Div. Gas Officer	
			All ranks were tested their helmets in Smoke + Gas	
			MUSTARD GAS in appliance + shown	
	13th		Reinforcements 15 2/L 21 ORanks. 2/L Roberts went to the area	

11 Bn Rl Wu Fusry Regt
for September 1917.
3

WAR DIARY
or
INTELLIGENCE SUMMARY

Army Form C. 2118.

Place	Date	Hour	Summary of Events and Information	Remarks and references to Appendices
	14th		of our attack to make themselves acquainted with the routes to be taken. Casualties 1 OR wounded	
	15th		Bttn. Operations on Training Grounds W 21. Batn parade 9.45 AM march to WALTON CAMP Area, GODEWAERSVELDE. 4.30 PM men marched well, no one fell out.	
	16th		Move continued 10.45 am to METEREN arrived 5 PM. Move further continued 9.45 PM then Trans continued 10.45 PM then tubac. another resting M 5 & 5.5 arrived 1.45 PM RENINGHELST WOOD CAMP	
	17th		Kit Inspections Troops cheerful Can hear the practice Barrage	
	18th		Men resting Parade 8.35 PM proceed to RIDGEWOOD arrived 10.40 PM Details remain at WOOD CAMP and later proceed to CARNARVON CAMP	

WAR DIARY or INTELLIGENCE SUMMARY

11th Queens Royal Regt.
for October
Army Form C. 2118.

Place	Date	Hour	Summary of Events and Information	Remarks and references to Appendices
	19th		Batln. move to YORMEUIL at 2.30 PM. Preparation for tomorrows attack. Everything including motors & ambulances. 11PM Rain falling.	4
	20th		Dawn Barrage opens attack is started. Batln move to HEDGE ST 10 to 5 am move to a position in Reserve (yesterday's front line) Batln HdQrs CLONMEL COPSE. Enemy counter attack on two occasions during the day. Casualties 2 O.Ranks killed, 1 Officer 8 Officers wounded 213 O.Ranks. Reinforcements arrive at CINNEVON CAMP	8PM Conference
	21st (Monday)		Enterance move forward. Water given out. JAVA TRENCH 10 O.Ranks killed 1 Officer 36 O.Ranks wounded 50 SHK. Reinforcements arrive 1 Officer were up to take in our company wounded Siclek Benetts and remain with us until the morning of Oct 23rd the remnant of Gibson's died in supremacy Caualeba

WAR DIARY
or
INTELLIGENCE SUMMARY

(Erase heading not required.)

11th Queen's R.W. Surrey Regt
for September 1917

Army Form C. 2118.

Instructions regarding War Diaries and Intelligence Summaries are contained in F. S. Regs., Part II. and the Staff Manual respectively. Title Pages will be prepared in manuscript.

Place	Date	Hour	Summary of Events and Information	Remarks and references to Appendices
	22nd (cont)		Battn. less one Company (A) relieved and move to MICMAC CAMP. Casualties 1 O.Rank killed 1 O.Rank Wounded	
	23rd	9.30 AM	Remaining company relieved move to MICMAC CAMP arriving 9.30 AM. Shields party also arrives Casualties 1 O.Rank wounded	
		2.30 PM	Battn return at ZUYDCOOTE	
			Delivered & marched to HALLEBRUCK area V.22 c 2.8 Moving articles replaced	
	24th & 25th		Troops rest Kit Inspection	
	26th	6.30 PM	Battn travelled by busses UXEM	
	27th	8.30 AM	Battn marched to ROSENDAEL (Fort de Dunes) arrived 9.30 AM	
			Under canvas on the Sand Dunes (nr the Sea)	
	28th		Had Adjut & Coy Parades	

WAR DIARY or INTELLIGENCE SUMMARY

11th Division R.W. Surrey Regt.
Army Form C. 2118.
for September 1917.

Place	Date	Hour	Summary of Events and Information	Remarks and references to Appendices
	29		Coy Parades = Bayonet fighting, Musketry (Fire Control) Bathing. Passes granted to DUNKERQUE	
	30		Church Parade in the Dunes. Bathing. Men learning swimming lessons.	

Potter Lt Col

WAR DIARY or INTELLIGENCE SUMMARY

Army Form C. 2118.

11"(S) Bn The Queen's
P.W.S. Regt
123/41
Vol 1 8

Place	Date	Hour	Summary of Events and Information	Remarks and references to Appendices
Fort de Dives	Mon 1st		Bn Bath at Fort de Dives in Coast Defence. Sandbagging round tents	
	2nd		Practice stand to all positions manned company in rotation — 2½ minutes from last Post. M. O.C. Coast Defence Lt Col Parr assumed hospital duties and (graduated round at Ypres) 4.16.4.17	
	3rd		Company on the beach all day	
	4th		Entertainment offered by General Hill — his Coast defence races cancelled W Battalion Old orders cancelled	
	5th		Relieved from Coast Defence by Lancaster Fusiliers. Marched to St Isidore 11.30 AM arrived 6.15 PM. Very hot day. Sager the night in new camp	
	6th		Day — motion Physical La (2nd Australian gunning Corp) 10.0 AM indent Col. Yorkshire Coast With Bore retired to Mendlesham 2/Lt W Brown	
			to Brigade as Intelligence Officer Reinforcements 2 Officers	
W.T.H B.F.O Fresney	7th		Sunday	
	8th		Officers visit front line. Company training	
	9th		C.O. Pole to Garrison Lt Col Garnett of Brigade Major E.C. Bowden MC. OC Rattn	
	10th		Company training — for rest	
			Grenade course Cpl engagements further bombs on the line under Capt 2rb Davis	
	11th		Bn.R.F Hq. Parade to Sette Old 11th but time football in the afternoon	

WAR DIARY or INTELLIGENCE SUMMARY

Army Form C. 2118.

(Erase heading not required.)

Place	Date	Hour	Summary of Events and Information	Remarks and references to Appendices
	11th		March out fire (Nos 5 Platoons attacked Lunette's) Casualties 1 O'Rourke Killed 2/Ranks Wounded. Trench Opponents Bivouac Sect 12.5J M20 —	
	12th		Fire Control Cream of Shitting Grenades Afternoon progressive enemy Churches located his dust B.H.Q. Casualties Wounded O'Rourke H Troops Inspection carried out. Entrainé alone the portion of the trench	
	13th		Casualties Killy O'Rourke Numerous slightly shelled but ours also shelled Casualties nil	
	14th		Enemy Quel Ing U=1146 Batn less 5 Platn returned by 2.30 Royal Junction. Draft. 1 Platoon remain with the 2nd Australian Tunnelling Coy continue to dig at trench Casualties Wounded 97 & Y Battn Wright to LaPanne & lighter over a couple of the extreme Sheet M.52 The Officers drilled on its tour	
La Panne	16		Troops clean up. Hot inspections Anti Aircraft Guard Mounted Kept inspection.	
	14th		General under Coy arrangements Rifle Kit & Bath. lens 1 Platoon lat	
	18th		Bath Parade for Bayonet fighting Physical Training Coy Drill Winners ? held at Casualties D Coy O'Gorman Rourke	
	19th		Gold Practice on M range LA PANNE Pay Parade Lewis Gun (Anti Aircraft) fired 1 magazine at Enemy plane 10.30 P.M.	

WAR DIARY or INTELLIGENCE SUMMARY

Army Form C. 2118. (3)

Place	Date	Hour	Summary of Events and Information	Remarks and references to Appendices
LA PANNE 	20th		10.30 AM Bombing practice at enemy aircraft flying rather low. Numerous attempts to see unlisted alarm during the night	
	21st		Coys scrubbing L.16. 3 Platoon Hay Saturday YMCA afternoon. Football match between Coys	
	22nd		Church Parade	
	23rd		Batt. Sandbag fatigue. Casualties D Coy Wounded O.R. in M.1 Coys ... half day. Also conducted Grenade Course Sandbag huts. Bombing Officer training parties	
	24th		Casualties D Coy Wounded O.R. 3. Bombers Rifle Bombers team Bombardment Coys Bayonet fighting Physical training afternoon Y Total	
	25th		Rifle & hand G Competitions (Platoon) Bombardment Day Platoon with Lewis + Stokes gun	
	26th		Coys march to training area. Field practice 2 Companies	
	27th		Attending Coy Butts Court Martial Rifle Bombers afternoon Officer on Batt. Vickers/B.P. 1 P's. Bombing afternoon 11 AM to 5 PM	
	28th		Regt Church Parade, Communion Service Coy Day relay as breakfast	
	29th		5 Platoon attacks to Australian Coy refugee came Batt sleigh to move to new Coy - Batt. party on land & up in Camp all Officers the Commen reached from tour	

WAR DIARY or INTELLIGENCE SUMMARY

Army Form C. 2118.

Place	Date	Hour	Summary of Events and Information	Remarks and references to Appendices
	30th		Battn. inspected by C.O. Coys. turned out full marching order. All is now complete but that regimental transport. All tr. is reduced to minimum weight for travelling purposes.	
	31st		All sand bags completed. All men attached to 2nd Battn etc return with B.E.F. then returning from leave.	

Awards M.M.
11652 Pte J. Bandle 20/2/1917
11407 " W.H. Clarke 24/9/14
6876 " K. Adam 24/9/14

M.C.
2/Lt C.T.M. Page 24/9/1917

E.A. Rowden
Major for
O.C. 11th Queens Regt.

www.ingramcontent.com/pod-product-compliance
Lightning Source LLC
Chambersburg PA
CBHW081527160426
43191CB00011B/1698